CARL THEODOR DREYER'S **GERTRUD**

THE MOVING WORD

This book is published with the assistance of a grant from the McLellan Endowed Series Fund, established through the generosity of Martha McCleary McLellan and Mary McLellan Williams.

University of Washington Press

P.O. Box 50096, Seattle, WA 98145, U.S.A.

www.washington.edu/uwpress

Library of Congress Cataloging-in-Publication Data

Schamus, James, 1959–

Carl Theodor Dreyer's Gertrud : the moving word / James Schamus.

p. cm.

Includes bibliographical references and index.

ISBN 978-0-295-98854-2 (pbk. : alk. paper)

1. Gertrud (Motion picture) I. Title.

PN1997.G433S36 2008

791.43'75—dc22

2008012317

The paper used in this publication is acid-free and 90 percent recycled from at least 50 percent post-consumer waste. It meets the minimum requirements of American National Standard for Information Sciences—Permanence of Paper for Printed Library Materials, ANSI Z39.48-1984.

CARL THEODOR DREYER'S **GERTRUD**

JAMES SCHAMUS

A MCLELLAN BOOK

UNIVERSITY OF WASHINGTON PRESS   SEATTLE AND LONDON

IN MEMORIAM

CASEY FINCH (1957–1994)
and
WILLIAM NESTRICK (1940–1996)

"Song made in lieu of many ornaments"
—SPENSER

CONTENTS

ILLUSTRATIONS

ACKNOWLEDGMENTS

The thanks I give for help with this little book are all out of proportion to its modesty and length, but not out of proportion to the enormous debts of gratitude I owe. On a separate page I dedicate this work to the memories of William Nestrick and Casey Finch, but their names bear repeating here. Many of these pages got their start in the dissertation on Dreyer I wrote at the University of California, Berkeley. Charles Tesson and Michel Sandras provided early inspiration and guidance. The English department at U.C. Berkeley and the American Scandinavian Foundation provided research grants for study in Copenhagen. There I was made welcome by the kind staff of the Danish Film Institute, under Ib Monty's direction, under the guidance of library staff Karen Jones, Lars Ølgaard, and Tim Voldsted. Peter Schepelern and Martin Drouzy shared their homes and their encyclopedic knowledge of Dreyer and Danish film with me. My colleagues and students at Columbia University have provided a wonderful home since for my ongoing work in film history and film theory. At Focus Features and, earlier, at Good Machine, my coworkers have put up with many irregular hours and preoccupied "phasings out" when I have disappeared into my research and writing. Particular thanks go to Ang Lee, David Linde, Andrew Karpen, and Ted Hope. Peter Kujawski shepherded the dissertation through my hectic schedule with unfailing good humor and skill. First Janelle Troxell and then Elise MacAdam provided expert research support; Vina Tran and Felipe Tewes helped in the preparation of the manuscript, and Amanda Doxtater assisted with crucial research and translations from Swedish sources; her work was greatly facilitated by Mats Cronwik, Magnus Blomquist, and Ida Poulson. Craig Knobles shared his translation of Söderberg's play with me. Jytte Jensen and Mary Lea Bandy at the Museum of Modern Art invited me to help with their catalogue on Dreyer and first put into print my early thoughts on him, some of which are reprinted here by permission from *Carl*

Th. Dreyer © 1988 The Museum of Modern Art. And Nelson Moe, Adam Bresnick, David Levin, Michael Levine, and Daniel Purdy—the Hunt and Theory Club—read chapters and provided crucial (if my sodden memory serves) help. Jeffrey Knapp, Charles Musser, Edith Kramer, Steven Nichols, Emily Anderson, and Peter Bowen provided help at various points along the way, and Jacqueline Ettinger patiently and expertly guided me through the publication process. Catherine Gallagher gave the final push that returned me to Dreyer and my dissertation. My doctoral committee—Mark Sandberg, Richard Hutson, and Julia Bader—provided painstaking and patient oversight. But it was the chair of my committee, Carol Clover, who inspired, and endured, the most. Two things are certain of this book: it can never meet her high standards, and it owes its entire existence to her. Finally, thanks to my three muses, Nancy Kricorian and Nona and Djuna Schamus.

CARL THEODOR DREYER'S **GERTRUD**

WHY A BOOK ABOUT *GERTRUD*?

The great Danish filmmaker Carl Theodor Dreyer's fourteenth and final film, *Gertrud* (Palladium, 1964), is easy to both praise and damn with the same breath; it is, after all, a perfect exemplar of that awful category, the "minor masterpiece." Awful, because, like its brethren (Raul Ruiz's *Three Crowns of a Sailor*, Billy Wilder's *Ace in the Hole*, and Abbas Kiarostami's *Close-Up*—the list could go on for pages and pages), we must admit about *Gertrud*: few have seen it, and of those who have, few love it. And yet. For, we might say, it is the quality of the love of those few that is so remarkable. From Jean-Luc Godard to Lars von Trier, from Paul Schrader to David Bordwell, *Gertrud* has trans-fixed the passionate regard of filmmakers and critics with a peculiar power of fascination, a fascination not unlike, I shall argue, that which Gertrud herself holds for her many failed lovers.[1] As the last great work of a filmmaker who himself sums up the oddly quizzical critical status of the *cinema d'auteur*, an auteur who appears to disappear into his own, often stylistically quite radically different films, *Gertrud* acts as a kind of cinematic vanishing point: we can claim that a powerful strain of modern European film practice organizes itself around it, but it is in and of itself not an object subject to vision—it is rarely cited, revived, or celebrated.

With this little book I hope, of course, to correct that general oversight; but I also, perversely, want to cherish the reasons for it. Even more perversely, I

---

1   For more on the film's reception, as well as a detailed look at Dreyer's work of adaptation, see Morten Egholm, "The innovative and wilful [sic] adaptor—What Carl Th. Dreyer did to Hjalmar Söderberg's *Gertrud*," *TijdSchrift voor Skandinavistiek* 27, no. 2 (2006), available from http://dpc.uba.uva.nl/tvs/vol27/nr02/art09. See also Paul Schrader, *Transcendental Style in Film: Ozu, Bresson, Dreyer* (Cambridge, MA: Da Capo Press, 1988) and David Bordwell's magisterial *The Films of Carl-Theodor Dreyer* (Berkeley: University of California Press, 1981). Lars von Trier has announced that he is making a documentary about *Gertrud*: available from http://www.hollywood.com/celebrity/Lars_von_Trier/190003.

would love to somehow preserve *Gertrud*'s relative invisibility even as I try to spread the reflected glory it radiates. To celebrate *Gertrud* is to praise paradoxically the ultimate cinephilic fetish, for we all know that what the cinephile most loves is the unseen and unseeable ("You mean you haven't seen Ozu's silent comedies? Even better than his fifties films!" . . . "I've got a bootleg of the subtitled French version of *La jetée*—I can't believe you've only seen that terrible version with the English voice-over!"). *Gertrud* is a film that goes right to the heart of that terribly sad—and transcendently liberating—love of the unseeable and unknowable object that is the cinema itself.

That is why writing a monograph about *Gertrud* is such a daunting task. The genre of the film monograph is supposed to provide the reader with something of a sustained reading of the film at hand: themes, motifs, production history, the place of the work in the filmmaker's career, a bit of gossip, the synopsis, an account of the form of the film, and the major influences that shaped it. There's some of all of that in the following, but not as much as you'll find in other movie monographs. In fact, this is something of an antimonograph monograph: I propose here something I hope you'll find even more in keeping with *Gertrud* as both film and idea; instead of a straightforward reading, scene by scene, of the film, this essay is a meditation—a collection of reveries, digressions, and extended footnotes and excurses—inspired not so much by *Gertrud* as by a single moment in *Gertrud*, a moment (or scene, or image—I'm purposefully rather loose about defining it) that has engaged my interest as exemplary of so much of what makes Dreyer such a disturbing and inspiring figure: his lifelong researches into the relations between word and image in film; his obsession with female martyrdom, and the ways in which his heroines enact and embody the struggle between text and picture—the *paragone* between painter and poet, as Leonardo da Vinci put it—that fueled so much of Dreyer's creative output; the unnerving mix of high-art aestheticism and grotesque violence that marks so many of his films; the way his narratives, from his earliest journalistic writings on the cinema to his last film, revolve around the quest of his characters to "read" and comprehend their own stories, a hermeneutic adventure that inevitably leads to moments of sublime incomprehension and often lethal catharsis; and, finally, the ways in which all of these motifs circle back to Dreyer's own biography, or figure as fragments of a kind of autobiography, which, as the great Martin Drouzy has shown, Dreyer obsessively figured in his search for the mother he never knew, a poor Swedish woman he could only imagine through his readings of the paper trail left by her short, tragic life—a life interrupted by Dreyer's illegitimate birth and subsequent adoption by a Danish family, which ended three years after she gave him up, when she poisoned herself in a futile attempt to abort another child.[2]

That she died a few short miles from the home of the real woman on whom the character of Gertrud is based—a home Dreyer visited while preparing the film and that he insisted be meticulously recreated for the last scene of the film—should not surprise us. Dreyer's journey there was both literal, as he pursued his usual intensive research into the "real" characters who underwrote his fictional ones (and he himself, as "Carl Theodor Dreyer," son of a Danish printer, was in so many ways a fiction), and figural, as he continued the endless journey back to his origins, to a place made up of words (parish documents, birth certificates, etc.) and the acts of imaginative creation and belief that might bring those words to life.

The moment in *Gertrud* that will serve as my jumping-off point is not a particularly dramatic or engaging one; I suppose I could have chosen from among hundreds of other moments in the film for a point of departure. (Perhaps, after reading this book, you will return to the film and discover your own place in which to meditate and from which to wander.) But it does, however slyly, tease us with the promise of deep meaning, by its rich melding of possible references. It happens to occur almost exactly halfway through the film, as *Gertrud*'s eponymous heroine turns to regard a large, dramatic tapestry hanging on a wall behind her. The tapestry depicts a forested landscape, in the center of which stands a naked woman, attacked from all sides by a pack of hounds (fig. 1). For all its sexualized violence and massive scale, the image on the tapestry is oddly calm, "aestheticised" one might say. Gertrud, after regarding it, turns to her friend Axel Nygren, who is also pausing over the tapestry's

2   See Maurice [Martin] Drouzy, *Carl Th. Dreyer né Nilsson* (Paris: Cerf, 1982) for a full account of Dreyer's autobiography.

1 "I had that dream": Gertrud and Nygren before the tapestry, in Carl Theodor Dreyer's *Gertrud* (Denmark: Palladium Films, 1964). Film still courtesy of Palladium A/S.

spectacle, and who is in the film one of a slew of masculine suitors—lovers, friend, and husband—who negotiate with Gertrud for her love, and tells him that she had had "that dream"—referring to the tapestry—the previous night. Soon thereafter, Gertrud will sing Schumann's setting of Heinrich Heine's "Ich grolle nicht" to her assembled admirers, accompanied on the piano by her current faithless lover, only to collapse in a swoon before her impossibly desiring audience, having just learned from another ex-lover that her current one had publicly boasted of their affair the night before at a soiree attended by lowlifes and whores.

In this book, we shall travel to many of the places that Gertrud's gesture toward and into the forest depicted behind her will take us—and often travel quite far afield, to the text buried, we might say, in the tapestry, and to the ways in which that text comments on, and is commented upon itself, by Dreyer's film. Along the way we shall encounter a number of interlocutors—Joan of Arc, Leon Battista Alberti, Gotthold Ephraim Lessing, Boccaccio, the French turn-of-the-century psychiatrist J. M. Charcot (as well as some of the patients he housed in his asylum and displayed onstage during his weekly lectures), and others—but we shall always circle back to the pregnant moment when Gertrud recognizes her dream in the tapestry on the wall in that parlor.

"Pregnant moment" is itself of course a term of critical art—we shall trace its roots back through Lessing's important work on the relation of word and image in the arts, *Laocoon* (1766), to see how Dreyer's use of the tapestry challenges our received ideas on how narratives find their ways into and out of images. But the term also carries a host of other meanings and associations, associations that will lead us into an extended detour back to another one of Dreyer's heroines, Joan of Arc, and into the history of the iconography of that heroine's depiction, a history that directly bears upon Gertrud, as well as upon Dreyer's own mother, Josephine Nilsson.

IF *GERTRUD* IS SUCH A GREAT FAILURE, HOW IS IT SO GREAT?

Gertrud, like the performance by Gertrud that follows the moment we've chosen, was an abject failure. Its premiere at the Salle Médicis in Paris on December 18, 1964, was covered by the Danish press as a national humiliation (even the Danish ambassador to France posted an account in *Kristeligt Dag-blad* the day after the screening, lambasting the film). Hopes for the film had been high: Dreyer's previous film was the masterpiece *Ordet* (Palladium, 1955), which had won the Golden Lion for best film at the Venice Film Festival when it premiered there in 1955, and Dreyer's return to Paris for the *Gertrud* premiere marked an auspicious return to the scene of another of his masterpieces, *The Passion of Joan of Arc* (Société générale des films, 1928). Although *Gertrud* recovered somewhat from its initial critical drubbing (young critics like Jean-Luc Godard and André Téchiné soon rallied behind it, and *Gertrud* even ended up winning the Bodil Award the next year for best Danish film), it was a commercial failure, treated by the public as a stilted, dated, lugubriously paced swan song from an old man (Dreyer turned seventy-five during the making of the film and would die four years later), based on a respected and periodically revived but not overly admired turn-of-the-century stage play by the Swedish writer Hjalmar Söderberg. And, indeed, the film *is* stilted, it *is* slow-moving; its pleasures, to those few who have yielded to them, are not only hard-earned but perversely painful. Of course critics and cinephiles have always found in cinema's "bad objects"—those films that bravely take on and subvert the reigning codes of American-dominated classical film narrative construction—a way to transmute the pain and exhaustion most viewers feel when subjected to them into the exquisitely transgressive experience we have come to identify with modern connoisseurship.

The salutary power of that transmutation has inspired much of the criticism of *Gertrud* to date; indeed, *Gertrud* is a perfect case study for turning artistic "failure" into—or, rather, for accepting a kind of artistic failure *as*—the precondition for another kind of aesthetic achievement. The groundwork for understanding that kind of achievement-through-failure was made by Immanuel Kant some 200 years ago in his third *Critique*, where he outlines the experience of the sublime—as opposed to the beautiful—as the result of a kind of cognitive failure, a shock to the system, when we initially fail to ingest the limitlessness presented to us in specific moments of experience.[1] In the experience of the sublime, our initial failure and displeasure (at the headache induced by trying to get to the "end" of an infinite progression of numbers, for example, or at the initial recoil of witnessing the overwhelming power of nature's might) is followed by the exhilarating feeling of having experienced something that, by definition, is greater than anything our faculties could ever allow us take in. For a long time now Western high-art practice has lived under the shadow of the sublime: the aesthetic became the "anti-aesthetic"; great works of art are now by definition "minor," for what artist would have a chance of getting into the Whitney Biennale with something trivial or kitschy enough to be called "beautiful"? Better by far for the artwork to stage a kind of unpleasant failure, thus generating in the beholder the struggle to grasp the greatness of the concept the artwork enables.

Recent thinkers have attempted to revive the legitimacy of the beautiful within art practice and theory. The wonderful critic Dave Hickey, for example, has passionately defended the photographs of Robert Mapplethorpe precisely for the transgressive power of their beauty.[2] I think a study of Dreyer's *Gertrud* has a lot to say to these current debates about the sublime and the beautiful, about the very definition of the work of art and the role of art in our lives. Dreyer's project in *Gertrud* represents, on the one hand, a serious engagement with the profound legacy of Kantian sublimity, as that legacy is extended and

1 Immanuel Kant, *The Critique of Judgement,* trans. James Creed Meredith (Oxford: Oxford University Press, 1952).

2 Dave Hickey, *The Invisible Dragon: Four Essays on Beauty* (Los Angeles: Art Issues Press, 1994).

transformed from Hegel through Jacques Lacan to current thinkers such as Slavoj Žižek. I have no doubt that its "failure," its "minor" status, is very much entwined with Dreyer's (and his heroine's) uncompromising quest to move beyond the confines of cinematic "art" to something more frightening and true. On the other hand, *Gertrud* is also a work deeply preoccupied with the aesthetic. As critics of *Gertrud* have repeatedly noted, the dominant presence of aesthetic objects in the film, and the contemplation of them by the film's characters—along with, of course, the hyperaestheticised feel of the entirety of the film's framing and staging—makes the film peculiarly "beautiful." It is as if Dreyer's fixation with art and artworks in *Gertrud*, and his characters' tragically unceasing failure to connect with their beauty (or, even more tantalizingly, their heroically tragic *rejection* of beauty), created the conditions for what we might call Dreyer's beautifully sublime aesthetic.

That aesthetic was a function of Dreyer's radical form of realism, a realism very different from what we usually associate with that word. Dreyer was not interested in mimesis, the faithful imitation in art of some version of our shared reality. His realism does not have the same social or political mission often linked to the Scandinavian and other realists who preceded him. The "Real" that Dreyer attempts to achieve in *Gertrud* and in many of his other films functions in some ways as the sublime did for Kant, and is even more like the "Real" as it is understood by Lacan and Žižek, as a structuring but largely ungraspable ground of our very being as human subjects.

We noted above the link between Dreyer's search for his own origins and, in the process of creating *Gertrud*, his final return to the home of the "real" Gertrud, the closed door of which would become the last image of the film—the last image Dreyer would ever produce (fig. 2). In creating his art, Dreyer sought, and portrayed his characters as seeking, a Real that is both the limit against which the human in us must throw itself to achieve self-definition, and the unknowable territory it is our moral duty to map, even if only by demarcating the borders we always try, and always fail, to breach in order to arrive there. The door onto that reality was always closing to Dreyer, and will always be closed to us—Gertrud herself closes it, and closes herself behind it. But *Gertrud* attempts, always, to pass into and beyond the frame filled by that

2 Frames and doorways: The final image of *Gertrud*. Film still courtesy of Palladium A/S.

image of the door. It is precisely the failure of *Gertrud*'s words and images to cohere in that attempt—precisely its failure as "art" of a kind—that marks the grandeur of Dreyer's ambitions: *Gertrud,* as much as any other film I know, ruthlessly argues the case against art, even its own art, and instead proposes a new kind of painful aesthesis, an aesthetic knowing, born of the rending and opening up of the human subject as it confronts the making of its own life story. For Dreyer, self-knowledge means creating one's self as an object of self-regard, but in that act of self-creation lies the rub: we are folded back into the falsehoods of aesthetic objecthood, and the abyss of constant interpretation and self-reflection. As we shall see, *Gertrud* both embraces absolutely this process of self-aesthetisization, and, finally, rejects absolutely its beauty in the name of the Real.

WHAT DOES THE "REAL" HAVE TO DO WITH THE *GERTRUD*'S "TALKINESS"?

Failure, then, is of the essence when speaking of *Gertrud*, itself the story of a failed marriage, a failed adulterous affair, and a failed attempt to redeem and perhaps rekindle an earlier love. Or at least that's how the men in Gertrud's life see it. Part of the enduring seduction of the play, written hastily by Hjalmar Söderberg after he fled to Copenhagen from Stockholm following the dissolution of his affair with Maria von Platen, is Söderberg's willingness, for all his anger at his truculent ex-lover, to grant, indeed to celebrate, her rejection not only of him but, seemingly, of any entanglement that might obstruct her quest for a love impossibly free of its object.

The plot of Söderberg's play is fairly simple, and Dreyer, in his adaptation, makes it even more so. The film commences in the parlor of Gertrud's home, as Gertrud and her husband, the soon-to-be-named government minister Gustav Kanning, discuss their failing marriage, as well as the arrival in town of a former lover of Gertrud's, the poet Gabriel Lidman, who is to be honored the following night at a banquet at which Kanning has been asked to give a toast. Kanning's domineering mother visits. Gertrud begs leave to go to the opera (Beethoven's *Fidelio*, of course). But instead of going to the opera, she meets her young lover, the handsome and gifted composer Erland Jansson. Kanning, on the spur of the moment, goes to the opera house to join Gertrud, whereupon he discovers that Gertrud never arrived there. At the banquet the following night, Gertrud takes ill and removes herself from the party to an adjoining salon, on whose wall is hung the tapestry of the woman and the hounds. She is joined in the salon by her old friend Axel Nygren, who has been away in Paris studying the newly fashionable field of psychiatry. He gives her a pill for her headache ("All the artists in Paris take it," he says) and she feels somewhat better; the two of them discuss free will, make note of the tapestry, and Nygren tells her a bit about his psychiatric studies, which include hypnotizing a woman who has a "sixth sense."

As the banquet ends, Gertrud's husband Kanning finds her. He tells her he knows she lied about going to the opera, and even though their marriage is a sham he demands she spend one last night with him. He goes off for a bit, and Gertrud is now joined by her ex-lover Lidman, who alternately implores her in anguish to tell him why she deserted him years ago, while also informing her of a party he attended the night before in the company of the Stockholm demimonde, where he heard young Jansson boasting of his mistresses, Gertrud among them. Jansson arrives, and Gertrud is prevailed upon to sing to the small after-party. Jansson accompanies her on the piano. In the middle of the song she collapses.

The next day she meets Jansson in the park; she tells him her marriage is over, but he rejects her, admitting to another affair with a powerful woman who has helped along his career. Back at Gertud's house, Kanning takes a phone call, leaving Lidman in the parlor as Gertrud enters. She and Lidman talk, and she explains why she left him years ago. (As she explains, we see, in flashback, what caused her rupture—her discovery of a note he had scribbled to himself denigrating women's love as compared to man's work). Lidman departs, dejected, and Kanning reenters the room, begging her to stay in their marriage. She tells him she'll probably move to Paris, now that her lover has broken her heart. In despair, he tells her to go. She does, and he cries out after her. In a final scene, taking place fifty or so years later, Gertrud receives her old friend Axel Nygren at her country home, where he presents her with his latest book of criticism, an appraisal of Racine. He notes that she has not replied to his letters. They speak of their friendship, and of the importance of love. She hands him back the letters he has written her, and he tosses them into the fire. She then recites a poem she had written as a youth, and they discuss the inscription that she has decided upon for her tombstone: "Your name, I suppose?" Nygren asks. "No," replies Gertrud, "on it there will be just two words: *amor omnia.*" Love is all. They say their farewells.

As the above attempt at a synopsis indicates, *Gertrud* is an almost impossible movie to give a précis of, as, by movie standards, almost nothing happens in it—though by "real life" standards, the dissolution of a marriage, the end of a tragic love affair, and the rejection of another string of lovers surely counts as something. This disjunction, between a movie made up of "just people sitting around and talking" and a movie made up of more or less the most shattering emotional events an adult can conjure, provides the summa of a lifelong Dreyer problematic about language and—and *as*—action. Dreyer defended that problematic in a newspaper interview at the time of *Gertrud*'s release, relating it to the films of the French new wave:

We have long been aware that a film is supported by conventional expression and types. The new wave we have is an expression of desire by the young to break away from this convention. We must have new subjects, new forms of production. In *Gertrud* I have tried to find such a new film form where dialogue is in the foreground, and the picture slips more into the background.[1]

I am going to make much about this visualizing of the perspectival place of dialogue, of how Dreyer paradoxically imagines a single space for words and images to share, and of how the image recedes into its own vanishing point in this new, shall we say, con-text.

One formal strategy Dreyer employs to "slip" his images into the background is to elongate his shots over time, making them seem more like spaces, say, than "shots." The film lasts 111 minutes, but is comprised of only 89 shots. (To give you an idea of what this means, the average American film these days has something like 1,500 shots.) So when critics complained of its glacial pace and "theatrical" staginess, we can understand why. And it is, by any standard, dialogue-heavy, though the purposely leaden delivery of the dialogue makes of it something quite different from the spoken language we hear in most other sound films. This also makes the physical "actions" of the characters, however

---

1   Jean Drum and Dale Drum, *My Only Great Passion: The Life and Films of Carl Th. Dreyer* (London: Scarecrow Press, 2000), 257.

minute—sittings or standings, gazings or sightings—particularly eventful, or at the very least, events of some kind.

To choose, thus, a "moment' from such a film is to remark on something the status of which Dreyer himself was keen to problematize: Is a moment a "shot"? A still or frame? Is it a scene? Think of it this way. We tend to conceptualize, since Lessing certainly, images and the plastic arts in general as pertaining to the order of the spatial, while thinking of narration and dialogue, and the verbal arts in general, as pertaining to the order of the temporal. This was the central thesis of Lessing's *Laocoon:* the argument that the verbal and the visual arts were fundamentally different, and that certain modes of representation were proper to the arts of time while others were proper to the arts of space. Dreyer, by deliberately confusing these two orders—how does dialogue get put into a "foreground"?—is signaling a radical reconfiguring of Lessing's artistic borders. Dreyer understands that the cinema adds motion to pictures by projecting one still image after another, thus transforming a spatial art into a temporal one, too. But unlike Sergei Eisenstein, and the great structuralist and semiotic thinkers who followed him, such as Christian Metz, Dreyer does not analogize the unfolding of film's moving images as a kind of articulation, akin to language. Dialogue (even, as we shall see, dialogue in silent films) runs a kind of interference; language in *Gertrud* projects itself between picture and beholder, linking each over time, but also enforcing its own temporality, its own rhythm.

Thus, in *Gertrud*, a "moment" always partakes of these two kinds of temporality, as Dreyer plays with the discrete, particular, almost indefinable intersections of language and image that form the "events" and "actions" his characters' words bear witness to—"events" as opposed, say, to "monemes" or some other minimal unit of cinematic signification film theorists have long struggled to define and isolate.

Dreyer lets us understand the hybrid, mixed-up nature of even the most basic building blocks we use to understand movies. A moment may not be a specifically filmic construct, though we all understand the filmic currency of the idea when we see it reproduced so often, both in our own accounts of memories of films we've seen (like "Remember at the end of *E.T.*, where the bicycles are fly-ing?" or "One of my favorite moments is when Lauren Bacall tells Humphrey Bogart, 'You know how to whistle, don't you?'") and in the machinery of film appreciation ("The 100 Greatest Movie Moments!"). And while I don't wish to assign too great a methodological importance to this notion (though critics and theorists such as Robert Ray have made powerful cases for the kind of work it can enable), I do want, without apology, to luxuriate in a moment as Dreyer understood it, and to dream, perhaps a bit as Gertrud dreamed, the image and story of it.

Because that dream has as its "foreground" the words on which Dreyer based his film, our recognition of it will always act through a kind of citation. The entire film, of course, cites Söderberg's play, and the characters in that play constantly cite and recite various texts and stories. Gertrud, when seeing the tapestry, for example, witnesses, in real life, her dream; but her dream was not made up of a single image, and the image itself clearly cites some other text, too. The instant of her seizing, in vision, the tapestry, brings forth and stands for an entire narrative, and that narrative itself cites and stands in for yet another. There is a long path through the forest of images and stories along which Gertrud and the lady in the tapestry both ran before they reached that moment.

So before we begin our own journey into and through that moment, we would do well to follow Dreyer's own path toward it for a bit. It was a path he cut in his endless quest for what he called, in the same interview quoted on page fourteen, "individualization," the self-realization that happens when the words his characters speak can "stand alone" apart from such "incidentals as light and sound." This is the work of Dreyer's unique realism, for the particu-lar realism of Dreyer's lifework defined the tragic heroism of his characters: the realist character Dreyer constantly strove to bring to life—unlike, say, an allegorical figure in a mystery play—is precisely that aesthetic construct that demands to be more than a construct, more than a collection of phrases in a script. The Dreyerian realist character demands to be, impossibly, individually, "real," and the story she desires to cite is always, impossibly, her own.

When Inger, the dead mother of Dreyer's *The Word* (*Ordet*, 1955), is miraculously brought back to life through the simple, uncomprehending faith of her child—faith in "the Word" that the child's uncle cries out for over her casket— Dreyer found an almost too-perfect enactment of the animating power of art when it attains the status of word made flesh, and redeems the suffering of our incomplete selves. Nine years later, in *Gertrud*, his energies would turn in a more pessimistic, but no less sublime, direction as he contemplated the possibility that such union was simply an illusion, and the Word—and its accompanying regime of signification and claims to jurisdiction over the destiny of human experience—was a cruel and remorseless power that human beings must defy in order to live in true relationship to themselves and to reality.

WHY WAS DREYER SO FASCINATED WITH

THE "REAL" GERTRUD?

Dreyer's quest for a real basis for his own characters was never-ending.[1] With *The Passion of Joan of Arc* (1928), for example, Dreyer rejected the original, poetic script written for him by the French writer Joseph Delteil. Instead, he based his screenplay strictly on what he thought to be the actual records of Joan's trial, working closely with the historian who had recently reedited them. The opening shot of *Joan of Arc*, while probably the film's least memorable, is, in this context, its most emblematic: a hand flips through the pages of what are purported to be the trial transcripts, in which, the intertitle tells us, we can discover Joan "as she really was."

That shot establishes a rhetoric of realism based not on the transparency of the filmic illusions to follow but rather on the assertion of the film's respect for textual evidence, as it seeks to re-present the real spirit of its characters. This realism I call "textual realism," an aesthetic practice based on the authority of its documentary rhetoric.[2]

Just as Dreyer researched the "real" Joan, so in *Gertrud* Dreyer claimed that his heroine was not the Gertrud of Söderberg's original 1906 play but the real woman whom Söderberg himself fictionalized, Maria von Platen. Dreyer, who had many years earlier toyed with adapting some of Söderberg's other works, was inspired to make *Gertrud* after reading about the publication of a recent doctoral thesis by Sten Rein that uncovered von Platen as the inspiration for

---

1   The following account draws heavily on the work of Martin Drouzy, who traces the autobiographical component of Dreyer's desire for the "real." See Drouzy, *Carl Th. Dreyer*, 147ff.

2   James Schamus, "Dreyer's Textual Realism," in *Carl Dreyer*, ed. Jytte Jensen (New York: Museum of Modern Art, 1989).

Gertrud.[3] Von Platen also inspired the character Lydia Stille, heroine of Söder-berg's autobiographical novel *The Serious Game* (1912), another account of Söderberg's traumatic affair and the breakup that in real life sent him flee-ing Stockholm for Copenhagen. Dreyer incorporated a great deal of Rein's research, as well as his own, into his take on *Gertrud*, to significant effect.

This approach to his film adaptations was fully in keeping with Dreyer's nearly obsessional working methods during the final decades of his extraor-dinarily long working life. Odd as it may seem, Dreyer claimed that his adap-tation of *Medea* (eventually made in 1988 for Danish television by Lars von Trier) was "not directly based on the tragedy of Euripides, but . . . is an attempt to tell the true story that may have inspired the great Greek poet."[4] The true Joan, the true Medea, the true Gertrud—not to mention the true Mary, Queen of Scots, or the true Jesus, to whom Dreyer devoted nearly twenty years of painstaking historical research (even, in his seventies, learning Hebrew)—are all phantasmatic objects of a reality made tangible to Dreyer only through the artistic transmutation of documents into images.

Phantasmatic, too, in the fact that so few of them ever saw their shadows reach the screen: to visit the Dreyer archives in Copenhagen is like walking through the imaginary libraries of the blind Borges: file upon file of carefully typed or neatly printed notes, literally thousands if not tens of thousands of sheets, and books—whole specialized collections on Greece, early Christianity, and the Scottish Reformation—evoking an uncanny doubleness of purpose: the Dreyer archives are themselves Dreyer's archives, the archives of an archivist.

Dreyer's demand for the "real" posed challenges both thematic and formal, and in important ways mirrored his characters' own battles. For the archetypal theme of the realist text itself is the hero's attempt to transcend his or her own textual status—to become a consciousness. The realist hero—or, more often than not, heroine—is thus locked in a life-or-death struggle with the author who penned her, with the authority who controls the words. Dreyer, in con-

---

3   Rein's thesis was turned into a book entitled *Hjalmar Soderbergs Gertrud: Studier kring ettkar-leksdrama* (Stockholm: Bonniers, 1962).

4   Drouzy, *Carl Th. Dreyer*, 356.

stantly trying to "end-run" his authors—in Gertrud's case, Hjalmar Söderberg—tried to solve the problem of realism's exorbitant desires by aligning
himself with his heroines, and, in turn, aligning his heroines with their actual,
documentary sources, against their authors' fictional formulations. The "secondary" nature of Dreyer's late work (both *Ordet* and *Gertrud* are not only
adaptations from plays, but technically "remakes": *Gertrud* had been made into
a made-for-TV film starring Anita Björk for Swedish Television just over a year
prior to Dreyer's version, and *Ordet* had been adapted by Gustaf Molander in
1943, twelve years prior to Dreyer's version) reflects Dreyer's desire not to
make definitive interpretations of his texts but, through a kind of pilgrimage
to their original incarnations, to bring forth the reality they incarnate.

It is a process that the great realist theorist André Bazin celebrated in his
essay "Theater and Cinema—Part One."[5] My students are often puzzled by this
essay: how can a realist like Bazin, champion of Italian neorealism and enemy
of theatrical styles of cinema such as German expressionism, celebrate the
genre of filmed theater, especially theatrical adaptations that retain the flavor
of their theatrical origins and don't try too hard to make themselves adhere to
the conventions of cinematic realism? Bazin's answer is surprising: the "reality"
of filmed theater lies in its underlying text, and it is only by respecting the "dramatic primacy of the word," by refusing "the major heresy of filmed theater,
namely the urge 'to make cinema,'" that we can become present to the transcendent reality of the word.[6] Dreyer's final work fits perfectly into this understanding. Gertrud is "theatrical" precisely in order to be "real": putting the
play's text into the foreground is not simply a stylistic preference for Dreyer
but a way of preserving that text's link to the reality Dreyer always sought as
his greatest goal.

One odd consequence of this absolute fidelity to the idea of the primacy of
the text is the concomitant erasure it performs of the text's author. In *Gertrud*,
Söderberg's play is a way station to an even more "real" source, as Dreyer

---

5   André Bazin, *What is Cinema?* trans. Hugh Gray (Berkeley: University of California Press,
    1967), 1:76–94.

6   Bazin, *What is Cinema?* 1:86.

seeks a paradoxical return to a kind of "authorless" writing, something like the "authoritative text" that David Bordwell sees as governing the narratives of all Dreyer's films. This authorless text transcribes the assumption by its heroines of a self-authoring free agency, a speaking body that articulates its own intentions and truths, and it is probably no accident that Gertrud's own take on the question of free will occupies a central position in the moment we are about to consider. The anxiety of authorship is a central preoccupation of the "real" characters Dreyer always depicted, and Gertrud is no exception.[7]

7   David Bordwell writes on *Joan of Arc*: "This conflict reminds us that ironically the entire narrative depends upon the very record that the authorities kept; the book which existed solely to insert Jeanne's words into the court's circuit of exchange is now used to reactivate that circuit in the very projection of the film. The historically authentic trial text must be presented in all its frozen materiality if the principle which it represents is to be questioned, put in dialogue with the image's spiritual word. In a sense, the film's images become a cinematic gloss, a running commentary upon the trial record." *The Films of Carl-Theodor Dreyer*, 95.

WHY CAN'T IMAGES AND WORDS (AND MEN AND WOMEN) STAY MARRIED IN *GERTRUD*?

One of Söderberg's most important predecessors, the great Swedish playwright August Strindberg, had solved the problem of his characters' authorship in his own way, in his famous preface to *Miss Julie* (1888), by claiming that the human soul itself is nothing but a collection of texts: "My souls—or characters—are conglomerations from various stages of culture, past and present, walking scrapbooks, shreds of human lives, tatters torn from old rags that were once Sunday best—hodgepodge just like the human soul. I have even supplied a little source history into the bargain by letting the weaker steal and repeat the words of the stronger."[1]

Strindberg hoped to neutralize the powerful desire his "characters" have for "souls" by neatly conflating the two terms, as his narratives stage the "stealing" of his own words. For Strindberg, the tragic irony is that in the modern world the "weaker" beat out the stronger more often than not: the "characters" steal the "author's" soul. Perhaps the strongest figuring of such a "weak" soul is the vampire, a figure that haunted fin de siècle Scandinavian and northern European culture, most famously depicted in Edvard Munch's paintings. Strindberg sees the vampire as a "soul-murderer," a weaker soul who steals, through performance, the words that make up the soul of the stronger. In Strindberg's version of "source history," the author is vamped by his very own characters.

The vamp is of course a feminine figure, and the gender politics of Strindberg's take on realism are virulently misogynistic: "I say Miss Julie is a modern character not because the man-hating half-woman has not always existed but

---

1   August Strindberg, *Selected Plays*, trans. Evert Sprinchorn (Minneapolis: University of Minnesota Press, 1986), 208.

because she has now been brought out into the open, has taken the stage, and is making a noise about herself."[2] What Strindberg doesn't mention here, in his preface to *Miss Julie*, is that the tragic heroine of his play is in fact based on a real-life woman writer, Victoria Benedictsson. The threat of the half-woman is the threat of the writing woman, the woman who makes "a noise about herself." So too in Strindberg's play *Creditors*: the emasculating Tekla is a writer, her disarmed husband Adolf, a painter.

The theme of the emancipated woman in Scandinavian realist theater (it is above all manifest in Ibsen, for example in *A Doll's House* and *Hedda Gabler*) is thus not just a theme, but a textual matrix through which is figured a whole complex of formal and ideological concerns. Realism creates the desire for real characters—those of the "weaker sex" who struggle to produce language they can claim as their own—and so creates an internal tension about the adequacy of its own textual authority. (One could give a version of the story of the transmutation of the confident realism of the modern breakthrough in Scandinavian literature of the 1880s into the symbolism, romanticism, and decadence that followed by tracing the fissures that this tension created.)

In Dreyer, this realist desire for real selfhood is magnified to truly heroic proportions—and so too is its counterpart, the rhetoric of the authoritative, containing text. This battle between self and authority is often gendered. Indeed, virtually every film Dreyer made—from his first, *The President* (1918) to his last, *Gertrud*—takes as its theme the confrontation of women with the patriarchal powers that attempt to define and dominate them. Dreyer's insistent centering of the female heroine can thus be seen as a continuation of this realist thematic/formal matrix, and at the same time a modernist attack on the foundations upon which it was built. The narrativized "anti-text" traces the fate of the "feminine" subject as it confronts authorities not only male but, significantly, "textual": legal, religious, and artistic. Dreyer's men nearly always represent specific institutions that use language as a primary means of gaining authority and wielding power.

In *Gertrud*, Dreyer found a perfect way to depict that struggle. At one point

2 Ibid.

3 "Man's work and woman's love": Gertrud renders Lidman's image. Film still courtesy of Palladium A/S.

Gertrud recounts to her former lover Lidman, a poet, why she decided to leave him. We see, in flashback, how one day, tidying up the books in his apartment, she sits at his desk to write him a note. Picking up a piece of paper to write on she finds a sketch of her profile, scribbled by Lidman, with an accompanying motto: "Woman's love and man's work are enemies from the start." Furious, she grabs a photograph of Lidman and tears it in half (fig. 3).

The torn photograph signifies the irrevocable ending of their relationship, a divorce that, for Gertrud at least, was decreed the moment she spied her image sharing a page with Lidman's writing. The gesture of tearing a photograph is one that Gertrud's current husband Kanning will repeat only minutes later in the film, after Gertrud informs him that she is now leaving *him* — the torn photograph will be of Gertrud this time (fig. 4). The rending of the image, as a sign of — as, indeed, the very act of — divorce, registers the power of the vow even as it is broken.

Gertrud, like all of Dreyer's films, is a work of painstakingly composed images. But at the same time it is a work born of a profound distrust of the image,

4 **"Gertrud! Gertrud!": Kanning rips a photograph of Gertrud in half. Film still courtesy of Palladium A/S.**

almost, at times, a hatred. Some of this hatred is inscribed in Söderberg's play. Söderberg's *Gertrud* is explicitly organized around the failure of male speech to control the stage, a failure to situate the characters visibly, especially Gertrud herself. The play opens with Kanning's summons of Gertrud ("Gertrud!" is the first word uttered in the play), and ends with Kanning's tragically powerless re-summation of the departed Gertrud as the curtain falls: "Gertrud! Gertrud! Gertrud!" Dreyer didn't want his film to end on such a note of failure, and so he added an epilogue, depicting Gertrud as a serene old woman taking stock of her life. And in this coda, Dreyer will once again invoke the written word as the basis for his film's claim to realist authority: he sprinkles Gertrud's dialogue with words taken from an actual letter written shortly before her death by Maria von Platen, in which she gently dismisses a former lover, the critic John Landqvist (on whom Dreyer based the character Axel Nygren, another of his additions to the play). The "real" Gertrud's own words trump, at the end, the frustrated summons of her male author—in Dreyer's film, Kanning quixotically succeeds in invoking Gertrud's image back onto the screen, but her appearance comes well after he himself, and his author's text, have been removed, so to speak, from the picture. In *Gertrud*, the image is grounded in the text, but also in the failure of the text's author.

As one consequence of the power of this problematic over Dreyer's work, *Gertrud* becomes, by the end, as Charles Tesson justly puts it, dominantly a "mise en scène de la parole et du texte,"[3] a staging of language. The film's hesitant pacing, the theatrical weight of the characters' interactions, all have to do with Dreyer's insistent focus on talk. André Téchiné was the first to take note of the literal weight of the words in the film, the way in which they so heavily disengage themselves from the bodies of the protagonists, and how that disengagement itself becomes central to the film's drama.[4] Gertrud herself is a concert singer, whose failed performance before her private audience signifies the disjunction between verbal performance and image that makes her existence intolerable. All of her lovers represent some aspect of male verbal dominance: Kanning, the lawyer; Lidman, the poet; and Erland, the composer (who, as Dreyer knew, was himself based on a real-life writer, Gustaf Hellström). Even her soon-to-be lover and friend Axel Nygren is a literary critic. The impossibility for Gertrud of sustaining a relationship with any of her lovers—explained in the film as the result of the extraordinary demands her love places on its objects and the resultant decline in their ability to work, to produce texts—can be contextualized as an intolerance to writing. Indeed, in the final epilogue, when Axel visits the aged Gertrud and asks why she has never responded to his letters, her answer is to hand back the letters, and, quoting von Platen, to reprimand him for having written with a typewriter. Nygren responds by throwing the letters in the fire.

For Téchiné, *Gertrud* "makes visible the final stages of the acquisition of the order of language," dramatizing the "living movement" from which words become detached and with which those words "will never again merge."[5] This

---

3   Carl Theodor Dreyer, *Oeuvres Cinématographiques 1926–1934*, ed. Maurice Drouzy and Charles Tesson (Paris: Cinémathèque française, 1983).

4   André Téchiné, "La parole de la fin," *Cahiers du cinéma* 164 (March 1965): 72.

5   Ibid.

"making visible" of language's constitutive rupturing of experience—of the way we use language to make sense of our experience but in so doing alienate that experience's meaning into an abstract order of significance separable from our bodies—is what places the visual aspect of Dreyer's film under so much pressure. To the extent to which the characters "make sense" of their situation they also detach themselves from it. And when those moments of consciousness come, they are often accompanied by violent attacks on the images from which each particular character's consciousness detaches itself.

The languorous pace of the film, with its long takes and its characters' labored speech and actions, makes the attacks on the photographs all the more striking—they are the most violent actions in the film. To understand both the dramatic and the thematic importance of this violence, let us return to the specific scenography of Gertrud's iconoclasm: a woman is interrupted at her own attempts at writing by the appearance of her own image, and next to that image, a man (a writer) has written that his work (the work of writing) is forever at odds with her love. The writing and the image, which share the same blank space of the white sheet of paper, represent for Dreyer two different orders of being: a symbolic, verbal order he mostly associates with the masculine, and the visual realm of the image, most often coded as feminine.

For Dreyer, the space of the film screen was, like that sheet of paper, the site of an impossible marriage between these two orders. And the strange power of *Gertrud* lies precisely in the unresolved tensions between Dreyer's need for masculine writerly authority on the one hand, and, on the other, the transcendent claims of the image, whose power he figured as feminine.

WHY ARE DREYER'S IMAGES, WHEN THEY "QUOTE," SO OBSCENE?

If I have for the moment focused on Dreyer's iconoclastic hatred of the image in *Gertrud*, it is equally legitimate to focus, as does the critic Jonathan Rosenbaum in his perceptive essay "Gertrud: The Desire for the Image," on Dreyer's conflictual longing for the image. Rosenbaum, taking his cue from feminist psychoanalytic theory, aligns the image with a feminine, nonnarrative subversion of the masculine, verbally grounded order of the narrative. He argues that the nonnarrative elements of the film (which, for Rosenbaum, are therefore the visual elements) are as important to Dreyer as the story. The film's long takes undermine what drive the narrative might provide, establishing a space that takes on meanings separate from the manifest plot. Rosenbaum points out that "the obsessive desire for the image is as central to the meaning of *Gertrud* as the habitual desire for the story, and the furious, unceasing tug of war between these desires is the very source of the film's tragic rhythm."[1]

This tug-of-war between word and image is the dominant agon of Dreyer's career. The opening shot of his very first film, *The President* (1918), signals what was to be a lifelong issue. It is, like the first shot of *Joan*, a close-up of the book on which the film is based, as a hand flips through its pages. *Leaves From Satan's Book* (1919) carries in its very title Dreyer's bibliographic obsessions. And then there's *Ordet*, with its handwritten author's signature at the opening of the credits, and its central problematic of the individual's relation to the Holy

---

1   Jonathan Rosenbaum, "Gertrud: The Desire for the Image," *Sight and Sound* 55, no. 1 (Winter 1985–1986): 40.

Book and the Word it carries. As David Bordwell has pointed out, Dreyer relied on "the symbol of the book to signify the authority behind narrative representation."[2]

But, as we have seen, the book's authority, and thus the authority of the masculine order of things, is always at issue in Dreyer's films; he was as mistrustful of the word as he was of the image. For if Dreyer is famous for anything, it is for the intense emotionality with which his films portray the struggles of his heroines against the order of the word. In *Joan of Arc*, for example, Dreyer focuses his film solely on Joan's trial, on the questions and answers that passed back and forth between Joan and the scores of male judges who grilled her. Dreyer is not interested in showing Joan's heroic exploits, or her relations with the people, or the military and spiritual training she received from her "voices." The story of the film, told through Dreyer's famous orchestration of close-ups, is simply the single-minded and relentless quest of the judges to get the illiterate Joan to sign her confession. Her greatest crisis comes at the moment of her signature; and her martyrdom follows, the result of her renouncement of that writing. It is a martyrdom often staged by Dreyer's heroines. Siri, for instance, the heroine of the fourth segment of *Leaves from Satan's Book*, is a telegraph operator who dies rather than tap out a message for the evil communists who hold her children hostage. Her martyrdom—which takes the form of a refusal of forced writing—prefigures Joan's: Joan is sent to the stake for renouncing her signed confession. Marguerite Chopin, the vampire of *Vampyr* (1932), is uncovered through a reading of the book *Vampires*;[3] and young Anne, in *Day of Wrath* (1943), attempts to subvert the Bible itself in her openly sexual reading of the *Song of Solomon*. Her sensual subversions ultimately lead to her death at the stake.

2   Bordwell, *Films of Carl-Theodor Dreyer*, 29.

3   Mark Sanderson points out (in an e-mail to the author, April 20, 2003) that Chopin does not fill the same narrative role as Joan in Dreyer's work. She is a sinister perpetrator of violence. The point here is that her role as vampire is linked to the Strinbergian vamp by Dreyer's use of text as her ultimate foil. See also Bordwell, *Films of Carl-Theodor Dreyer*, 111ff, for a related argument regarding Dreyer's use of intertitles as "authoritative voice" in *Vampyr*.

Dreyer's heroines are constantly doing battle with authorial figures, and their "transcendence" is almost always a martyrdom at the hands of a textual regime. Gertrud renounces life with others because her love is too strong to tolerate her lovers' allegiances to their writerly careers—Gabriel and his poetry, Gustav and his law, Erland and his composing. Gertrud's last words in the film, to Nygren, are of a supreme irony: "And thank you for your book."

Joan of Arc, just like *Gertrud*, marks perfectly Dreyer's divided allegiance to his authorities and his heroines. Dreyer, as director, must "submit to the writer whose cause he is serving," as he once wrote of his own approach to adaptation. But, as always, that writer is not the author of the screenplay, but the real person, such as Maria von Platen, whose own written traces Dreyer would assiduously track down and reproduce. If, in *Joan of Arc*, this writing is always produced under duress (Dreyer, we recall, founded his film on the transcripts of Joan's interrogation and torture), in *Gertrud* Dreyer was still seeking for some way in which his heroine could write of her own "free will."

In this, Gertrud's proximity to Dreyer's own mother must have played a role. For Maria von Platen produced more than her letters: she actually had a son—a son she essentially abandoned when she walked out on the marriage arranged by her family to a man twenty-six years her senior. In the play, mention is made of the son as having tragically—if rather conveniently—passed away. (One would think this terrible loss would play more significantly in the drama of the piece, but it barely registers.) Dreyer erases all mention of the son in his film version (and Sten Rein pays scant heed to him in his book, though in Söderberg's *The Serious Game* Lydia Stille, the von Platen character, is depicted as having a daughter, and the male stand-in for Söderberg in that novel himself has a child out of wedlock, cared for by a foster family—a detail that would not have been lost on Dreyer). Martin Drouzy makes a convincing case for the haunting presence of this lost child—in essence, Dreyer himself—in *Gertrud*, noting how one day on set, when a reporter came to visit, Dreyer obsessively spent hours staging an incidental encounter between two extras—a reunion of a parent and child—on the steps of the opera house, as Kanning arrives looking for Gertrud. This small piece of background action had nothing to do with the plot, but to the reporter on hand it appeared to consume nearly all of Dreyer's attention that day.

The image of the lost parent and the production of the words that both erased and preserved her are emphatically conjoined throughout Dreyer's career, and in many ways Dreyer's life story uncannily mirrors that of Gertrud and his other heroines; his life, too, was a constant battle between word and image. His first profession was in journalism, and he began his work in film as a screenwriter and intertitle writer, gradually working his way up to director. And during a particularly long dry period in the thirties, when he could get no film work, he had to go back to journalism to support himself. Only a Danish government–sponsored job as the manager of a cinema saved him from a similar fate in the last years of his life.

Just as in his life, the book, the word, and writing in general all function in Dreyer's screenplays as both impediments to and necessary components of the art of filmic creation. It is this disruptive tension underlying his art that has made Dreyer's films so idiosyncratic and his place in film culture so difficult to pin down. For while his films are intensely visual, the experience of watching them is often an experience akin to reading, of interrupting the flow of filmic images, of slowing it down, of cutting or tearing it to make it legible. Their interest is as literary as it is cinematic in the traditional sense. This critical ambivalence before Dreyer's work—is it cinema or a kind of literature?—is strongly prefigured by the filmmaker himself in his own written responses to the cinema. An early example will suffice to show how.

In 1912, Dreyer, then working as a journalist in Copenhagen, made a visit to the set of a film shoot. He prefaces the article he wrote about his visit (one of his very first writings about film) with some general comments about the silent cinema: "When one goes to the movies to see a gripping film tragedy, one can hardly put off the thought that the dialogue, which one can't hear, is not always in complete agreement with the film's sad or solemn plot. If one could read the silent language of the lips, one would certainly experience a great shock, as did an American teacher of deaf-mutes," who, Dreyer reports, was forced to ban film screenings at his school for deaf-mute children after reading "the most obscene and meaningless words [Sjofelheder eller Meningsløsheder] on the lips of film actors, both men and women."[4]

Dreyer then follows up this observation with a humorous first-person account of his visit on the set, where, during the filming of a moving scene between two lovers, the hero orders lunch—some herring and a couple of beers—while the heroine tells him of her love for another.

What Dreyer fails to mention in his article is that the film he watched being shot was in fact based on a screenplay by none other than—Carl Theodor Dreyer. *The Brewer's Daughter* (1912) was Dreyer's first screenplay, and its success led Dreyer eventually to take up his first full-time film job, in charge of writing intertitles for Nordisk Film, at that time one of the largest and most successful film companies in the world.

Dreyer got into the film business by way of the written word, but he never really left writing behind. His career path would always be haunted by what he would figure as a crisis in representation, the crisis that occurs at the translation point between words and images. At that moment, the words become obscene and nonsensical, as the images take up and transform the meaning that once resided in them.

For Dreyer, the obscenity of that moment remains imbedded in the image, a mark both of the image's origins in language, in the screenplay, and of the image's freedom from the order of language. To "read" a film is to witness an affront to the authority of the word, to participate in the production of a story at once "solemn" and blasphemous. And such is the feel of Dreyer's films— they have an almost authoritarian weight to them, even as their meanings can be read as subversive or revolutionary. It is this mixture of solemnity and obscenity that makes Dreyer, even a hundred years after his birth, so difficult to figure out.

---

4   Carl Theodor Dreyer, *Tommen: Carl Th. Dreyersjournalistiske virksomhed,* ed. Peter Schepelern (Copenhagen: C. A. Reitzels Forlag, 1982), 19.

SO WHAT, AFTER ALL, IS THE TAPESTRY QUOTING?

Let us now turn to our chosen moment, and ask: what does the tapestry Gertrud regards have to do with the obscene presence of language in Dreyer's films? Let us first make note that the tapestry is itself preeminently a quotation—a visual quotation, to be sure—but a quotation nonetheless. It figures, in some way, Gertrud's dream of persecution: like a dream, it is not simply, as we noted above, an image but a story, a narrative of some kind. And, just as importantly, it quotes, in its *haute bourgeoise* way, as a reference to some prior text, some story which it figures forth—for we can assume that no fashionable turn-of-the-century Copenhagen parlor would display a depiction of such a horrendously violent scene without the representation being motivated and explained by its literary, "cultural" origins. As a tapestry, the image is itself a kind of weaving or text—a textile, a fabric of meanings, the "textus" from which our later idea of text as written composition emerges as a kind of rhetorical "figure"—that Western culture, at least since Homer's Penelope, has associated with the feminine, and in particular with the wife whose husband is not at home. Its weaving is an act of faith, but also an act of rejection—Gertrud, like Penelope, refuses her suitors in the name of a purer, more real love. But unlike Penelope, Gertrud includes in that rejected category even her husband. And this difference is what marks the difference, the rhetorical gap, between Gertrud's citations and the tragic irony of their meaning in the film. *Gertrud*, the film, as text, as a kind of weaving, mobilizes and embodies this "difference": it can itself be understood as a montage of tragically ironic citations of and commentaries on the celebrations of marriage that it, as we shall see, obsessively quotes.

The tapestry in the parlor is emblematic of this citational obsession. It plays as a bit of story business, while serving as a figure of at least one person's—

Gertrud's—interpretation of the narrative. But it prefigures the plot, too—in this case the scene just minutes later, when Gertrud will collapse under the emotional weight of her hangdog admirers. And it also functions in what might be called a postleptic fashion in regard to Gertrud's own, interior dream vision. Gertrud had already seen, at least in some sense of the term, the tapestry—or perhaps the story the tapestry references—before she looked up at the wall.

Like a musical number, the tapestry both slows down the plot, making the film's characters momentary spectators and readers, while at the same time relaying important narrative information. It is one of many moments in the film when the characters, and in particular when Gertrud herself, stops before a frame within the frame of the screen to pause and consider, to comment and interpret—indeed, most of *Gertrud*'s commentators and interpreters make of the film a kind of apotheosis of hermeneutic desire: statues, paintings, mirror images, tapestries, songs, poems—just about every aesthetic object imaginable is contemplated and interpreted in the course of the film by Gertrud and the other characters. One could argue, indeed, that the act of interpretation is one of the primary "actions" the film depicts.

But such interpretive acts are intimately connected with the violence that the image within the tapestry inscribes and offers. And like many of the most violent images in Dreyer's films, the scene on the tapestry is both straight-forwardly brutal and strangely serene. It is one of a long line of conflations in Dreyer's work where high art and low violence—in particular misogynistic violence—are identified as coefficient (and the "gynistic" aspect of the tapestry is hard to miss—the pictured woman's sex serves as the image's approximate vanishing point). Certainly, one would think, the depiction of such raw bru-tality could only be excused by the status of the depiction itself as "art"—and its status as art is itself dependent on its status as citation, as a woven image that is also in important ways a quotation of a verbal text. For Dreyer, though, it is perhaps precisely this textuality, and the aesthetic imperative it embodies, that makes the tapestry so brutal an object to behold.

This aesthetic imperative is given its discursive weight in part because the excuse, if you will, for the image is its function as a "quotation" of something, some mythical or literary episode in a classic work of Western literature, a reference to the kind of work with which the cultured people in *Gertrud* should presumably be familiar. Indeed, Söderberg, in his original manuscript page for the play, described the tapestry as having "mythological motifs."

Certainly, when I first pondered the image, one of my initial impulses was to ask: from what source does this scene come? To make the question even more interpretationally urgent, I should also make note that the scene on the tapestry is there by Dreyer's choice. In Söderberg's play on which Dreyer bases his film, Gertrud is framed by not one but two tapestries, a hind—not a woman—being ripped apart by dogs, and a depiction of the birth of Venus. Dreyer, in conducting the research that inspired his adaptation of the film, certainly came across a reproduction of Söderberg's original manuscript page describing the setting for the scene in the parlor (it was reproduced in Sten Rein's book), in which Söderberg had at first written "woman," then crossed the word out and replaced it with "hind." Dreyer decided to go back to Söderberg's literal, if you will, first intention, replacing his figurative substitution with the woman who stood there originally.

But who is this woman? Much to my chagrin, I could not immediately come up with the reference. At first, I could only recall images of a man, not a woman, being chased by the hunter's hounds, as when Acteon is turned on by his own dogs. When, I asked, has a woman been depicted in such a predicament? One would think, given the status of women in Western art and society in general, that such an image would be more or less ubiquitous. But examples were not easily forthcoming.

I did come up with a few suitable references for the tapestry, in particular book four of Virgil's *Aeneid*, where Dido is metaphorically pictured

like a wounded doe caught all off guard by a hunter
stalking the woods of Crete, who strikes her from afar
and leaves his winging steel in her flesh, and he's unaware
but she veers in flight through Dicte's woody glades,
fixed in her side the shaft that takes her life (IV, 92–97)[1]

---

1 Virgil, *The Aeneid*, trans. Robert Fagles (New York: Viking, 2006), 129–30.

While this fits Söderberg's revision (and interestingly references Gertrud's collapse as being analogous to Dido's erotic swooning), it is still a stretch when trying to justify the depiction of a fully naked woman being attacked by dogs. Its focus is on the ignorant state of Aeneas, the unknowing hunter who has wounded Dido by his simple adorable presence, and Dido certainly is not being attacked by hounds in the episode, although elsewhere in the poem she'll be strongly associated with Diana, goddess of the hunt, who is figured here as a hind.

Perhaps Dreyer, in making the change from his own source material, simply decided to humanize and sexualize the violence of Söderberg's image, to—with one obscene gesture—tear off its Aesopian alibi and reveal its ugly, violent truth. Whether or not that is the case (and it is a perfectly plausible explanation), we are still left to account for the dominant feel of the "citationality" of the tapestry, for the perfectly natural assumption it produces in us, its viewers, of its cultural legitimacy and legibility. In other words, whether or not the tapestry *has* a source, it *needs* one. For it is not simply an obscene and violent image, it is a "pregnant moment," as Lessing would say—a moment on the cusp of narrative fruition, on the verge of catharsis and closure—and we thus receive it as culled from some preexisting story, as exciting as our "looking forward" to the moment it tactfully precedes. (Even Dreyer, I think, would have demurred showing the scene, just seconds away, of the woman being ripped to shreds by the dogs.)

Lessing's influential argument, about just what moment from a narrative text it is appropriate to embody in a visual image, is more than relevant here. Lessing's great fear was of the unintended obscenity and illegibility of an image that depicts a story's climax; for example, he commends the stoic demeanor of Laocoön's face in the statuary group depicting his and his sons' death, because his face has not yet been distended by pain to the point where it could no longer properly signify his tragic fate. After all, the image of a face completely ruptured by screaming could easily be confused with one contorted by laughter. And on the other side of the spectrum, too gruesome a depiction of the violence about to be inflicted on Laocoön would cause in the spectator a reaction similar to witnessing the real thing, thus transmuting our response from cathartic appreciation into involuntary disgust, and collapsing the artistic *sign* into an obscene *reality*. The tapestry adheres to Lessing's aesthetic injunctions perfectly.

I thus continued the hunt for my mythical or at least mythological source. Quite by accident, in a seminar I took with Professor Steven Nichols, who was presiding over a study of the subject of ekphrasis, an answer to my search appeared—an answer that, as we shall see, was itself ekphrastic. Before we continue on to our source, we should, therefore, get a sense of what this term means.

IS GERTRUD AN *EKPHRASTIC* FILM?

"Ekphrasis" is usually defined as the rhetorical performance by which a work of literature attempts to imitate a work of visual art. In its earliest uses, such as in Homer or later in the *Rhetorica ad Herennium* or in the Elder Philostratus' *Imagines*, "ekphrasis" is a description of a work of art, but when done well, an ekphrasis becomes, as heightened description, a kind of substitution, replacement, or reenactment of the work of visual art.[1] To give you an idea, no one has yet to find any of the multitude of artworks described by the ekphrases in Philostratus' book—it's quite possible that none of them existed, or that they exist only to the extent that Philostratus succeeds in creating them out of words.[2] Given that the *Imagines* is considered the earliest surviving work of sustained art criticism in the West, and that it is made up almost wholly of extended ekphrases of works of art, this is worth pausing over. The *Imagines* is a wonderful little book, a sophistical tour de force that engages the battle between word and image from its very first words—by insisting on the under-

1 See Ruth Webb on the "striking divergence" of definitions of "ekphrasis" in art and literary theory. She points out that in early uses of ekphrasis, "works of art as a category" of ekphrastic description "are of no particular importance" (11), and that emphasis rather was placed on the ability of an ekphrasis rhetorically to create an image in the mind's eye. "Ekphrasis Ancient and Modern: The Invention of a Genre," *Word and Image* 15 (1999): 7–18. James Heffernan, one of the most influential writers on ekphrasis, makes, however, a good case for retaining the contemporary understanding of the term as "the verbal representation of visual representation" in *Museum of Words: The Poetics of Ekphrasis from Homer to Ashbery* (Chicago: University of Chicago Press, 1993), 19.

2 Norman Bryson, in "Philostratus and the Imaginary Museum," gives a fascinating account of the debates over whether Philostratus was describing actual or imaginary paintings, critiquing in particular a famous 1941 essay by Karl Lehmann that proposed to resolve Philostratus's inconsistencies by reconstructing the layout of the villa described by Philostratus as the gallery through which he walks and in which the paintings are placed. *Art and Text in Ancient Greek Culture*, ed. Simon Goldhill and Robin Osborne (Cambridge: Cambridge University Press, 1994), 255–83.

lying rhetorical identity of both: "Whosoever scorns painting is unjust to truth; and he is also unjust to all the wisdom that has been bestowed upon poets—for poets and painters make equal contribution to our knowledge of the deeds and the looks of heroes—and he withholds his praise from symmetry of proportion, whereby art partakes of reason [logos]."[3] ("Logos" is the same word translated as "word" at the beginning of John: "In the beginning was the word.")

Philostratus then proceeds to his series of extended ekphrases, pretending to teach a young boy about art by walking with him through a villa containing the collection of a wealthy connoisseur. He begins in front of a painting portraying the Homeric character Scamander. But instead of instructing the boy to study or contemplate the painting, the first thing Philostratus does is ask the boy to "notice" something that is not, at least in the physical sense, there: "Have you noticed, my boy, that the painting here is based on Homer, or have you failed to do so because you are lost in wonder as to how in the world the fire could live in the midst of the water? Well then, let us try to get to the meaning of it."[4] The boy's mental absorption into the image causes a citational "failure" that requires an aversion of his eyes from the canvas: "Turn your eyes from the painting itself so as to look only on the events on which it is based."

Philostratus then proceeds to describe the painting almost solely in terms of its diegesis, of the narrative it tells, asserting its coherence and meaning in the measure in which the painting succeeds in communicating the story from Homer's *Iliad*: "Now look again, it is all from Homer," Philostratus says, telling the story of Hephaestus's attack on Scamander after the death of Patroclus, and pointing out the details of the setting. As Philostratus continues with his description, however, his ekphrasis takes an odd turn: "But the river is not painted with long hair, for the hair has been burnt off; nor is Hephaestus painted as lame, for he is running. . . . In this Homer is no longer followed."[5] Astonishingly, Philostratus, in this first ekphrasis in this first work of art criti-

---

3   Philostratus the Elder, Philostratus the Younger, and Callistratus, *Imagines*, trans. Arthur Fairbanks (New York: Putnam, 1931), 3.

4   Ibid., 7.

5   Ibid., 9.

cism, concludes by emphasizing precisely the painting's *divergence* from its textual foundation. To think painting, to create its theory and criticism, Philostratus must first think text ("it is all from Homer") and then articulate the "difference" from the text that the image embodies. For a rhetorician and sophist such as Philostratus, this difference creates the laudatory space of painting's rhetorical possibilities. Painting tells both the story of its text and the story of its own telling.

The story of Narcissus tells, for Philostratus, just this truth. For when Narcissus becomes entranced with his own reflection, the lesson is not just about the perils of self-regard but also of the power of painting to absorb and transform the narratives through which we account our lives. "The pool," Philostratus writes in a later ekphrasis, "paints Narcissus, and the painting represents both the pool and the whole story of Narcissus."[6] The "truth" of the image consists of just this doubleness—its sameness to *and* its difference from the text—and Philostratus's insistence on both is neither an inconsistency nor a contradiction but the very ground on which this kind of truth can be experienced. Ekphrasis insists on the productive rupturing of the space created by the mutual mirroring of story and image. Its words create images even as they pretend simply to describe or "mirror" those images; and the images they mirror are themselves already, in some fundamental way, made up of words.[7]

Dreyer's Gertrud is indeed something of a narcissist in just this fashion. Throughout the film, Dreyer insists on placing her in front of the mirror, having her appear as a mirrored reflection, having her "see herself" in images like the tapestry, or on allowing us to see her doubled in objects like the statue of Venus he places her under in the park. All of these reflections, as in Philostratus, "paint" Gertrud, and represent both themselves and her story.

In all of these narcissistic reflections, there is for Gertrud, as there was for Narcissus, trouble brewing under the surface, for the ekphrastic mirror never reproduces an exact double. There is always a rupture, a difference, *inside the*

6 Ibid., 89.

7 Bryson links this movement in Philostratus to Jacques Derrida's "logic of the supplement." *Art and Text*, 267. While my own inclination is to link, as I do below, the ekphrastic to Lacan's and Žižek's notion of the "Real," Bryson's Derridean approach is also fruitful and just.

image itself, made up of the words its story tells. Was Gertrud's dream, for example, a citation of, or reflection of, the tapestry we see behind her? Did her dream tell the same story as the one the tapestry attempts to image forth? And if so, just what is that story? Was her dream limited to this moment in the story? And is the woman in the tapestry Gertrud, or someone else? If it embodies in some way a story, whose story is it?

Ekphrases functioned in classical juridical rhetoric in the same sphere as the diegesis—an ancient rhetorical term familiar to film theorists, the diegesis is that part of the rhetor's argument that reconstructs the story of the crime in such a way as to bring it to life for the jurors. Cicero, for example, prosecuted one of his most famous legal cases by constructing a spectacular series of ekphrases of works of art that he claimed the defendant had stolen. The absence of the art works (they had not been recovered) increased their rhetorical presence, as Cicero made them appear through his words, simultaneously giving legal weight to the paintings' physical disappearance. Once again, the creation of the image in words had as its precondition the erasure of the image from the visual field, as if, to see the text properly, one had, as in Philostratus, to avert one's eyes from the image in order to regard the text from which it derived its meaning.

But that text is always, it seems, itself ekphrastic. If, as Grant F. Scott points out, ekphrasis "begins as a special aspect of the epic, as a type of featured inset which nominally digresses from the primary narrative line"[8] by interrupting the story to depict an image, it paradoxically develops over time, in the discursive realms of art writing, into story itself. In Giorgio Vasari's *Lives of the Artists*, as Svetlana Alpers points out, "Vasari describes paintings exclusively in terms of narrative qualities."[9] And, as we have seen, Philostratus' *Imagines* imagines its images predominantly as echoes or frozen slices of narrative flows, laying the groundwork for later theories, such as Lessing's, of the pregnant moment.

8 Grant F. Scott, "The Rhetoric of Dilation: Ekphrasis and Ideology," *Word and Image* 7, no. 4 (1991): 302.

9 Svetlana Alpers, "Ekphrasis and Aesthetic Attitudes in Vasari's *Lives*," *Journal of the Warburg and Courtald Institutes* 23 (1960): 191.

So, oddly, an image that brings to life a prior text is described, by subsequent texts, solely in terms of the narrative recounted in the earlier text. Art historian David Carrier, for example, tries to fix this narrative-centered aspect of ekphrasis by explaining it in opposition to interpretation: "An ekphrasis tells the story represented, only incidentally describing pictorial composition. An interpretation gives a systematic analysis of composition. Ekphrases are not concerned with visual precedents. Interpretations explain how inherited schema are modified."[10] The distinction Carrier tries to make between ekphrasis and interpretation can quite easily be collapsed or strongly identified with the great art historian Erwin Panofsky's notions of iconography and iconology. In Panofsky's terms, the interpretation of an image requires an iconographic stage, past the initial sensory apprehension of the image, where the viewer makes sense of the work's references to the "themes and concepts," the "stories and allegories," which, by the time of the Renaissance at least, meant religious, literary, and other texts. If the visual form of the work is "'sensible' as the indirect reflection of visual data of the lived world, it is 'intelligible' as a reformulation of literary content."[11] Paradoxically, iconographical description becomes by its very nature a description of narrative or, at the least, of text, of doctrine. As we make sense of the image, description and narrative collapse into each other, and the work is understood to be citing and referencing the world through the lens of the textual; thus the description of the work becomes the account of the narrative it embodies.

And while the ekphrastic performance may be, within the logic of epic narrative, a digression from the narrative, it is in fact a digression *made up* of narrative, a moment when the moving images of the narrative often fold back into the narratives of their own production. (The *locus classicus* for this is, of course, Homer's account of the forging of Achilles' shield in the *Iliad*.) The ekphrastic takes its place along the border crossing between image and word, a crossing at which the battle between description and narrative often unfolds

10 David Carrier, "Ekphrasis and Interpretation: Two Modes of Art History Writing," *British Journal of Aesthetics* 27 (1987): 21.

11 Erwin Panofsky, *Studies in Iconology: Humanistic Themes in the Art of the Renaissance* (New York: Westview Press, 2001), 4.

and collapses into a confusing draw. The aesthetic strategy of a slow-moving film like *Gertrud*, which so regularly and insistently pauses ekphrastically over its images, allows the film to, in a sense, rhetorically mirror itself, as its characters also pause to read the enframed narratives that make up their story. Edvin Kau, in his detailed and empathetic reading of *Gertrud*, arrives at a similar conclusion when he argues that Dreyer's formal strategies make of the film a kind of single picture, but one that evokes what Kau calls Dreyer's "favorite trick": "at fremstille og tolke på én gang"—to depict and to interpret at the same time.[12]

It is through the collapse of description into narrative, and vice versa, that rhetoricity, and thus "interpretation," seeps back into Dreyer's ekphrastic enterprise. Ekphrases are not incomplete interpretations, or structured in opposition to the interpretive enterprise; they are, by their very nature, interpretive endeavors, articulating in their own ways readings and truths—indeed, often positing their own subjects as implied or explicit readers and interpreters. Pictured and picturing, the ekphrastic subject finds within it the seemingly paradoxical aspiration of simultaneously being seer and seen, image and interlocutor, and is thus doubled at the crucial moment of its coming into being as such. It is "all from Homer" but "does not follow Homer," just as Gertrud herself is all from Söderberg but does not follow him, as we can see even in this one little moment, where she acknowledges a tapestry crossed out at its origins by Söderberg but restored by Dreyer. And Dreyer's method here—to go to the first, "original" image also informs his conception of Gertrud herself.

Gertrud figures, as much as any movie made, the pleasurable and painful birth of the consciousness created through that movement back toward origins—structured as it is by the uneasy liberal arts unconscious of much of what Raymond Bellour has called the "unattainable" or "unfindable" text of the cinema itself, the way movies themselves are essentially uncitable and unquotable. (Indeed, the difficulty of "quoting" from a film lies at the heart of our own circling around this "moment" in *Gertrud*.)

But, at the same time, the image, for all its uncitability, presents itself as

---

12 Edvin Kau, *Dreyers filmkunst* (Copenhagen: Akademisk Forlag, 1989).

essentially a citation itself. As Bryan Wolf puts it, an understanding of ekphrasis is an understanding of the rhetoricity of the image, rhetoricity understood as essentially linguistic: "I tend to *read* the visual when I see it these days, and to suspect that seeing comes inscribed with the same cultural politics as saying."[13] Ekphrasis, according to Wolf, is a "seepage of rhetoric from the visual to the verbal." Grant F. Scott critiques Wolf's "furtive" rhetoric of ekphrasis, with its "unpleasant sense of residual drip."[14] In a few pages I will argue that it is in fact the literal obscenity of Wolf's notion of the rhetoricity of images that gives his argument its charge, and that this pornographic "residual drip" of the verbal/visual encounter is not a haphazard metaphor, but an acknowledgement that the conjoining of words and images has a genuine sexual politics, and that Dreyer's life's work, with *Gertrud* at its end, was a sustained meditation on that politics. It is in this way that we can understand *Gertrud* as, impossibly, an ekphrastic film; Dreyer doesn't simply "foreground" words in his final film—his background is made up of them as well.

13 Bryan Wolf, "Confessions of a Closet Ekphrastic," *Yale Journal of Criticism* 3, no. 3 (1990): 185.

14 Scott, "Rhetoric of Dilation," 302.

AT LAST, HERE'S DREYER'S PROBABLE SOURCE—
BUT DOES IT MATTER THAT WE FOUND IT?

So let us finally return to our search for that defining footnote, the source that Dreyer quotes with his tapestry. Here is one possibility: in the eighth story of the fifth day of the *Decameron*, Boccaccio tells the tale of Nastagio degli Onesti, a noble gentleman of Ravenna, who loves a girl from the even nobler family of Traversaro. She, naturally, spurns his advances. One day, while walking in the woods outside of town, a terrible vision appears to Nastagio: a knight in armor hunts down a beautiful naked young lady, who is killed and devoured by the knight's dogs. The knight tells Nastagio that he too was in love with a cruel woman, so much so that he killed himself. Now both she and he are condemned to the hell of repeating this scene every day—he as punishment for his suicidal blasphemy, she as punishment for her cruel and unfeeling heart. So Nastagio goes home and decides to stage a feast in the forest, to which he invites the young woman and her family to dine, right on the spot where he had seen the vision. Sure enough, the scene is replayed at the appointed hour, but this time Nastagio's cruel young love interest looks on. She immediately understands the moral of the spectacle and, terrified, agrees to marry Nastagio on the spot.[1]

Thematically, we are on ground very similar to Dreyer's. Gertrud is nothing to her lovers if not unattainably cruel, but in a modern, sort of divorced, way— the film is, to a certain extent, the painting of her grounds for divorce, a divorce from romantic love itself, as well as from her husband and lovers. The image of the woman attacked by the hounds is first a kind of dream image, and then becomes embodied as artistic production—and in both texts this takes place

---

1   Giovanni Boccaccio, *Decameron*, ed. Vittore Branca (Turin: Einaudi, 1980), 420–26.

at a big banquet. But whereas in Boccaccio the theatrical spectacle of maiden-murder is first envisioned and then impressarioed by a man and leads directly to the theatrical spectacle of marriage, in *Gertrud* it is a woman who sees the spectacle first, as interior vision, only to be confronted by it again in the form of scenic decoration. Here, in its modern incarnation, it seems only an objectification of Gertrud's understanding of the perils of marriage itself, not an exhortation to stay married.

But perhaps the greatest citational "irony"—to use the term in scare quotes for a moment—that Dreyer's quotation of Boccaccio invokes is that it is a visual rendering of Boccaccio's decidedly verbal text. It produces for vision what was originally a verbal rendering of an event figured as primarily visual.

Before I go on with some of the interpretational consequences of all this, I want to flag one more irony. We now have a "source" or reference for the tapestry, that is, a prior, culturally sanctioned text whose story appears to be imaged forth on the wall behind Gertrud. It fits both in terms of some of the important visual details and clues (although I have been more than a bit selective in not mentioning some of the details Dreyer leaves out), and in terms of the thematic and narrative motifs the two texts have in common; and we can even assume that Söderberg himself, Dreyer's immediate source, might have intended or known of some of these links. (After all, where did Söderberg come up with the image to begin with?) And, finally, by noting the difference between the original text and its new use in Dreyer's work, we can clear out a discursive space where we can attribute meaning to the specific choices of selection and quotation Dreyer has made.

All well and good, except for one small nagging question: does the relatively "minor" nature of the text we are citing really "justify" its use in the film, especially when we consider the macabre and sexually charged violence of the image? Virgil is one thing, but the eighth story of the fifth day of the *Decameron* is another. In other words, even if we have succeeded in establishing a citational link, to what degree does that link really account for or "motivate" the textual and visual disturbance caused by the tapestry?

The relative triviality of the citation, and the pedantry it enables, are, I would argue, part and parcel of its Dreyerian excessive violence. It is excessive, in other words, not because it exceeds the textual but because it so slavishly *is* the textual. The murderous vision is justified if not by its specific footnote then by its simple gesture to the bibliographic apparatus, to the "cultural" as the site (or rather "cite") where icon and graphic become legitimately iconographic, where the image becomes legible.

IS DREYER QUOTING BOTTICELLI?

We find that Dreyer has as an iconographical precursor in his encounter with Nastagio no less an artist than Botticelli, who made in 1484 a series of paintings depicting Nastagio's story and spectacle—a series of paintings made not as individual canvases, but, appropriately, as panels meant as wedding gifts to adorn the home of a newlywed couple, akin to the paintings often made on the sides of the traditional Venetian wedding casket (figs. 5 through 8).

Here again, the occasion as well as the subject is marriage, and more particularly the relation between marriage, violence, and spectacle.[1] The four panels tell their story in chronological order. In the first panel, Nastagio sees the lady being chased by the knight on horseback and his dogs. In the next panel, the knight disembowels her as Nastagio stands watching in horror. In the next panel, the scene is replayed for the assembled banquet guests. And, in the final panel, Nastagio is married.

Notably, within each of the first two panels, multiple moments in the narrative are depicted within a rigorously organized perspectival space—a wonderful example of what Lew Andrews has called "continuous narrative" in his remarkable *Story and Space in Renaissance Art*.[2] While the space depicted is a single, unified field, it is inhabited by multiple moments in the story. In the first panel, for example, Nastagio appears twice, moving through the woods, from left to right, and again, "later," practically stabbing the fleeing woman as

---

1 For an account of some of the social conditions that caused such anti-feminist representations to flourish in the wake of Boccaccio's writings, see Ellen Callman's "The Growing Threat to Marital Bliss as Seen in Fifteenth-Century Florentine Paintings," *Studies in Iconography* 5 (1979): 73–92.

2 Lew Andrews, *Story and Space in Renaissance Art: The Rebirth of Continuous Narrative* (Cambridge: Cambridge University Press, 1998). Thanks to Anne Friedberg for this reference.

5 The source: Nastagio's forest. Sandro Botticelli, *Story of Nastagio degli Onesti* (first panel), Museo del Prado, Madrid. Reprinted by permission from Erich Lessing, Art Resource, New York.

she rushes from right to left. In the next panel, as she lies prostrate in the foreground, her entrapment is again depicted, in a kind of flashback, in the background, as she moves from left to right. Boccaccio's narrative, as a temporal unfolding, envisions the perspectively organized space as containing multiple narrative instances; the story does not simply bridge our movement from one panel to the next, as if, in a proto-cinematic montage, Botticelli were editing his images by linking scene to scene. For, especially in the first two panels, the pictorial space is itself broken up by the action of the story depicted within it. Andrews argues convincingly that the depiction of such multiple narrative moments within a single space is not some medieval holdover from preperspectival pictorial practices. Instead, he shows that our current thinking about perspectival representation is shaped by later developments, such as instantaneous

6 One space, many moments. Sandro Botticelli, *Story of Nastagio degli Onesti* (second panel), Museo del Prado, Madrid. Reprinted by permission from Erich Lessing, Art Resource, New York.

photography, which have led us to conflate single-point perspective with the depiction of single instants. Quattrocento artists and audiences, however, had no such expectations, and easily accepted the depiction of multiple narrative moments within single frames.

But looking again at the progress of the panels, we do see a distinct movement toward a more emphatically perspectival and unified depicted space, as the actions become more theatrically staged and ritualized—and reduced, indeed, to single "moments" viewable through a kind of proscenium theatrical fourth wall. From panel one to two we note an increased emphasis on the vanishing point reinforced by the placement of the (trimmed) tree trunks to frame the action within the panel's frame. In panel three, depicting the banquet in the woods, we see in the foreground that the trees have actually been chopped

7 Staging the story: Nastagio's banquet. Sandro Botticelli, *Story of Nastagio degli Onesti* (third panel), Museo del Prado, Madrid. Reprinted by permission from Erich Lessing, Art Resource, New York.

down to better our view of the action. And, in the final panel, Botticelli moves the action to a hall or loggia, whose architecture reinforces a rigorous perspectival centering, and where the only remnants of the forest are the decorative wreaths that adorn the pillars. Civilization replaces nature; marriage orders and structures the sexualized violence of the wilds. Significantly, the theatrical architecture of the proscenium itself has now taken center stage, with the human actors relegated nearly to the wings. The wedding ceremony replaces the violent and disorderly vision of the forest with the inscription of a sexual and visual regime in which the narrative excesses of the earlier panels can be resolved into the orderly perspectival logic of the final panel, a resolution that also collapses the representation from multiple moments into a single instant.

The course of Nastagio's own gaze, and his relation to it, mirrors this meta-

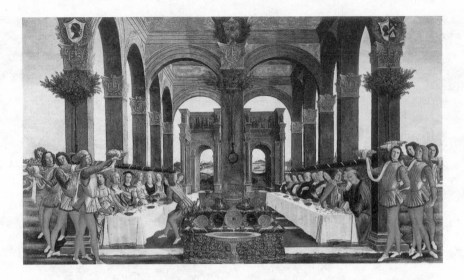

8 **Perspective and marriage. Sandro Botticelli, *Story of Nastagio degli Onesti* (fourth panel), private collection.**

story of the triumph of the perspectival. He begins with a moping, downward gaze, which is only roused to spectatorship by the violence winging its way toward him, and by his stance holding the hooked branch that clearly implicates him in the sexualized violence being staged in the forest. In the next panel his body recoils from the scene even if his eyes are glued to it, while when the actions are repeated at the forest banquet in the next panel we see his horrified gesturing transformed into a showman-like posturing, in which he addresses the crowd, narrating the story while calming his guests.

With his marriage goal achieved in the final panel, Nastagio's gaze, now directed toward his bride, becomes eccentric and particularized. There is no relay of glances in this final scene between Nastagio and his audience, no central focus for the crowd gathered within the frame, as there was in panel three; but our own gazes are emphatically directed to a plain central pillar, adorned by a circular bull's-eye, into which our vision is instructed to disappear. The panels tell the story of a vision split into story and scene, with one gaze multiplied and particularized into the characters' various points of view, and the other invited into the perspectival vanishing hole, around which the story-world is made finally to cohere. It is a proto-cinematic movement that resolves the violence of the spectacle into our gaze's marriage with the spectacular itself.[3]

Gertrud, of course, provides no such resolution. Rather, as in the moment we have chosen to study, it deploys and presents insistently emphatic single-point perspectives, while figuring its characters as eliding from, no matter how fascinating, the lure of its vanishing points.

Even *Gertrud*'s tapestry, reducing as it does Nastagio's story to a depiction of just one horrifyingly "pregnant" single moment, dramatizes this refusal of the marriage of spectacle and gaze. The rupturing force of its violence, even toward the story from which it is derived and which it "quotes," is magnified by one of the oddest things about it: the woman, rather than attempting to flee the dogs or beat them back, stands motionless, her left arm lifted to her face, her vision calmly preempted. At the moment of her dismemberment and death, she refuses to see the scene before her, assuming a gesture of calm mourning instead, directing her vision inward—much as Dreyer insisted on what has been called Joan's "faraway gaze" as a refusal between the traffic of language and image in *The Passion of Joan of Arc*. (Dreyer has her insistently eliding the eye-line matches that would normally link her image to those of her judges; in most movies, when a character glances off screen, we cut to what she is looking at, but in *Joan* such glances rarely cue cleanly motivated cuts). So, too, here the woman in the tapestry refuses to see the narrative about to rend and destroy her.

The tapestry pictorially describes its scene, but in doing so it makes that scene function in an array of narratives, many of which are narratives, implicit or explicit, of the interpretation of the scene by the film's different characters. The tapestry is pregnant with meaning, too, in another particularly perverse

---

3   The resolution of these prodigiously multiple gazes ties nicely into the point Christine Olsen makes in her essay "Gross Expenditure: Botticelli's Nastagio degli Onesti Panels." Linking the scene to the "endlessly recapitulated" murder by hounds of the two spendthrifts in Canto XIII of Dante's Inferno, Olsen argues that "over-indulgence"—gastronomical, financial, and amatory — is the main theme of the pictorial narrative. The final panel depicting the marriage, and, "likewise, the presentation of all four paintings at the conclusion of the nuptial sequence, when the bride was settled in the groom's house, imposes a coherent, persuasive interpretation of the entire ritual's constituent parts." *Studies in Iconography* 5 (1979): 165.

way: while in Nastagio's story it is one moment in a narrative of *marriage*, in Gertrud that moment is ripped from its reconciliatory origins and made emblematic of its heroine's commitment to *divorce*. By monumentalizing and isolating this one moment from Nastagio's story, Dreyer also radically reconfigures its status as story: for "divorced" from its originary context it can hardly be said to remain "Nastagio's" story at all, a story whose vanishing point has been reincarnated from the abstract bull's-eye of Botticelli's final panel into, it appears, the naked woman's sex.

As in Philostratus, the tapestry is "all from" its literary source, while staging a radical departure from its underlying text. Gertrud is herself the "difference" between the two. She sees herself inside the tapestry; she "had," in her dream, the story of it, and she now stands within Dreyer's frame, her marginal presence before the tapestry's frame a guarantor of its meaning within the film. What is the significance of Gertrud's dual perspective on the story, of her presence both inside and outside the tapestry? To answer that question we must occupy ourselves for a few moments with the scene's relation to the originary document in the modern West's embrace of perspective itself, Leon Battista Alberti's *On Painting* (1435). For central to Dreyer's project in *Gertrud* is the way Western perspective inscribes its own textual "other" into the vision it organizes for and proposes to us, the way that what we have come to think of as simple realism is in fact a very complicated negotiation between image and word.

WHAT IS DREYER TEACHING US ABOUT THE HISTORY OF PERSPECTIVE, AND HOW IS *GERTRUD* SO INTERESTING A CONTRIBUTOR TO THIS TOPIC?

We tend to think of Alberti's *On Painting* as being exclusively concerned with the arrival and demonstration in the West of single-point perspective; and indeed, few works in the history of Western culture can be said to have had such an impact on pictorial practice as Alberti's. But in fact the topic of perspective takes up only the first of the three "books" that make up Alberti's work, which has a great deal to say about just what kind of paintings Alberti believes perspective should be put in the service of.

If the past few decades have seen an avalanche of "ideology critiques" of Albertian perspective (its creation of the illusion of a centered, bourgeois subjectivity, and of a regime of "realistic" representation that naturalizes a dominant and dominating gaze), it is because the elegance and influence of Book 1 have assured it a pride of place in subsequent discussions of *On Painting*. I don't want to take issue here with the larger ideological arguments leveled at Alberti and the "realism" associated with his legacy (there's a great deal to be learned from them), but I do want to explore for a bit some of the complications those arguments may miss when they ignore the rest of Alberti's book, and show how Dreyer, in *Gertrud*, inspires a different approach to the Albertian legacy.

First, we should note one of the peculiarities of what happens to the scene of painting when Alberti arrives there. Albertian single-point perspective shapes the space of a given picture plane through the creation of the "pavement," the receding checkerboard floor, whether represented in the painting or not (fig. 9), whose presence transforms the blank surface of the painting into something more—into, indeed, one might argue, something that Western painting had a

9 Empty pavement. Fra Filippo Lippi, *Banquet of Herod*, Duomo, Prato, Italy. Reprinted by permission from Alinari, Art Resource, New York.

hard time depicting before Alberti: emptiness. Before Alberti, a painter commencing work faced a blank *surface*; with the arrival of Albertian perspectival construction, the painter faced an empty *space*. Alberti's answer to the question as to what should fill that space might surprise modern readers; rather than fill it with, as he put it, a "colossus" of figures and shapes, Alberti argued it must be filled with something of a different order altogether—with narrative, with an *istoria*, a story, or, as it is sometimes translated, a "history." For Alberti, it is the *istoria* that is the "great work of the painter," and much of *On Painting* is taken up, in great detail, with the nature of this task for the visual artist.

But stories need tellers, and so, "[i]n an *istoria* I like to see someone who admonishes and points out to us what is happening there; or beckons with his hand to see; or menaces with an angry face and with flashing eyes, so that no one should come near; or shows some danger or marvellous thing there; or invites us to weep or to laugh together with them. Thus whatever the painted persons do among themselves or with the beholder, all is pointed toward ornamenting or teaching the *istoria*."[1] Thus, at its very inception, "realistic" perspectival practice incorporates the ekphrastic into its technology of representation, filling the empty space it creates with language and narrative. And that language never completely finds a home there, erring, as it must, between depiction, margin, and text, requiring a "commentator" both inside and outside the painting.

Gertrud is an extended meditation on the emptiness of Albertian space, and on the constituent disconnect between word and image that emptiness always calls on us to overcome as we try, from the margins, to fill it with story. The film's characters are constantly moving in and out of frames—doorways, mirrors, windows—and, as Gertrud does before the tapestry, they continually serve as their own Albertian "commentators," parsing over significant moments as they themselves traverse in and out of the story spaces they create, as they vacillate between either side of the Albertian proscenium fourth wall inside and outside the stage of the play they enact. As David Bordwell has pointed out, *Gertrud* places an "unprecedented emphasis on doors, the passages into and out of the chamber. . . . One out of every five shots begins with an opening door or a vacant doorway."[2] He identifies this emphasis with the "theatrical" quality of the film, with the notable number of entrances and exits Dreyer's characters make. It is theatrical, too, in the way it highlights the proscenium, and thus perspectival, staging of so much of the film. Gertrud and her lovers enter and exit the movie continuously, but they also hover about it, peer into it, regard it, discuss it. Hence the feeling too that Gertrud's character is vaguely divorced from the proceedings she walks through.

Gertrud, and the film that tells her story, perform that divorce again and again by insistently splitting and refocusing her gaze (and ours) into fragments of pictorial space that reframe her relationships into multiple, if frozen, circumscriptions. This ongoing reframing is everywhere in the film: in the photos Gertrud and Kanning tear apart in anger; in the mirror filled with Gertrud's

---

1   Leon Battista Alberti, *On Painting*, trans. Cecil Grayson (New York: Penguin, 1991), 78.

2   Bordwell, *Films of Carl-Theodor Dreyer*, 173.

57

WHAT IS DREYER TEACHING US ABOUT THE HISTORY OF PERSPECTIVE?

image beside which Lidman addresses her; in the framing rectangular fireplace that looms dead-center in the image of Gertrud and Nygren sitting near the end of the film, whose light is fueled by the burning text of Nygren's letters; and in the film's last image of the door frame through which Gertrud finally disappears—the list could go on and on.

These framings create "aesthetic" spaces within the film, spaces that introduce an ekphrastic reverie into the larger space of their reception by the film's own characters. This reverie, reinforced by the film's "heavy" and slow dialogue, the "weight" of the texts its characters utter and play out, makes the characters' work an ekphrastic response to their own gestures and poses a central part of the film's narrative. Again, Bordwell has pointed out the proliferation of aesthetic objects within the film, noting that the film "uses art works to pose the problem of how aesthetic discourse can adequately represent the motive force of the narrative."[3] This problem—the adequacy of "aesthetic discourse" to "narrative" (and vice versa, we might add)—Bordwell rightly inflects as crucially concerned with "motive force," that is, with the assumption by the film's characters of intentionalities that can propel the events of the narrative forward. Specifically, Bordwell underscores the "persistent problem of representation" in Dreyer's films as "that of a relative independence of narrative logic and cinematic space and time."[4] While Bordwell emphasizes the defamiliarizing "emptiness" of the film's long pauses and vacant framings, "its prolonging our perception beyond narrative needs," he recognizes that this emptiness is also a "negative gesture," an "excess" that is "related to the inadequacies of narrative motivation."[5] At the end of this essay I will return to the significance of this "excess" in Dreyer's conception of his film texts. For now, though, I would only like to mark a small difference with Bordwell by understanding the "emptiness" he rightly sees in the film not as a kind of antinarrative void, but as exactly the ekphrastic space required for the dialogue between image and text to jointly create the stories they embody and tell. Just as Alberti, at the very birth of the

3 Ibid., 175.

4 Ibid., 176.

5 Ibid., 186.

empty space created by perspective, breaks the frame that defines that space by placing a commentator both inside and outside of it, thus allowing for the image to be filled with narrative as the commentator beckons our gazes; just as earlier, Philostratus imagined pictorial space as the scene of a story articulated in the sophistical theater of interpretation staged both in front and inside of that space; and just as Lessing imagined the difference between the visual and the verbal sign by making the visual image itself a "moment" of an unfolding verbal narrative; so too Dreyer places his characters in the margins of their own story-space, in order that they might participate in the creation and interpretation of their own stories.

Gertrud's scene in front of the tapestry, when read in the light of Philostratus, Alberti, and Lessing, brings to life a whole, often neglected, history of Western perspectival realism and the narratives that haunt it. Dreyer did more than simply go back to both the "original" woman in the image that Söderberg crossed out and the "original" Gertrud, his painfully researched Maria von Platen. He also figured their encounter with each other through a very specific rewriting of Söderberg's play at just this moment in its unfolding. For example, in Söderberg's play Gertrud is visited as she sits before the tapestry by a spectre of her teenage self, who reads to her a poem about love she had written at the age of sixteen; Dreyer will remove this text and have the aged Gertrud read it herself in the epilogue he added. Dreyer instead takes this scene as the moment to introduce a whole new character, Axel Nygren, who, as I mentioned earlier, is based on the real-life critic John Landqvist. Landqvist and von Platen had carried on a years-long affair; they met in Paris, where she had fled after the semipublic scandal in Stockholm of her break with Söderberg. The affair with Landqvist also ended in disappointment, but decades later Landqvist would write to von Platen, sending one of his books of criticism to her, on the occasion of her eighty-sixth birthday, and it is von Platen's reply to him, one of her few extant letters, that Dreyer uses as the basis for the epilogue he added to the end of the film. It was in Sten Rein's book that Dreyer came upon that letter, as well as a few others von Platen had written half a century earlier. Dreyer studied Rein's book carefully, taking copious notes on it and following up with further researches of his own based on Rein's leads, and Dreyer made careful note of Rein's depiction of von Platen's strongly independent character, which influenced Dreyer's own conception of Gertrud.[6]

Shaping the scene, Dreyer also cut significantly from the play's dialogue in front of the tapestry. (Dreyer's film has only about half the dialogue of the play, so the edits, especially of a number of bit parts portraying various shallow members of the Stockholm bourgeoisie, are not surprising.) It is, however, Dreyer's major *additions* to the dialogue here that we should now make special note of.

6   Rein argued strongly for von Platen's, and Gertrud's, dominant "hysteroid" emotional composition. I shall shortly return to this issue of Gertrud's "hysteria," and how Dreyer interpreted it.

WHAT DOES PERSPECTIVE HAVE TO DO
WITH FREE WILL?

The brief exchange that Gertrud and Nygren have about "free will" is particularly significant, as Dreyer has Gertrud approve Nygren's belief in free will in contradistinction to the grim fatalism of her father, who, she says, taught her that everything was predetermined. She makes her point by quoting words her father used to tell her: "You do not choose your destiny any more than you choose your wife or your children. You get them, but you do not choose them." But, significantly, what Dreyer has Gertrud quote in this scene are not words from her father, but words adapted from dialogue in Hjalmar Söderberg's novel *The Serious Game*.[1] *The Serious Game*'s main female character, Lydia Stille, is, as we have already noted, also based on Maria von Platen, but it is not she who is given this advice in the book by the newspaper editor Markel; it is Arvid, the semiautobiographical stand-in for Söderberg, who is on the verge of marrying a woman he doesn't love. And Markel is a complicated choice for the character to give such advice. "Markel," Söderberg writes, "was a bachelor, involved in an old unhappy love relationship with a woman who was no longer young, but nevertheless young enough to deceive him with almost anyone"[2]—a woman, in other words, very much like Gertrud. Markel functions in *The Serious Game* as a secondary, paternal image of Söderberg himself, here giving his younger self the bitter advice born of his own Gertrud-like relationship.

In having Gertrud articulate her belief in free will by quoting from, and rejecting, words spoken by a pathetically paternal version of Söderberg from

---

1 Hjalmar Söderberg, *The Serious Game*, trans. Eva Claeson (London: Marion Boyars, 2001). Thanks to Amanda Doxtater for pointing this out.

2 Ibid., 84.

his novel about her, Dreyer creates the perfect example of Strindberg's "walking scrapbook," a character arguing for its own self-determination by quoting its own author (here figured as her "father"), against, Dreyer could perhaps imagine, that author's very own intentions.[3] It is a declaration of independence from her "source," but made through words provided by him, very much like the image in the tapestry behind her, an image both excessive to but grounded in the text that motivates its presence.

The very ground of Gertrud's existence, as a willing, desiring self, is staked in this tragic twilight zone between fictional and real selfhoods. In a terrible and moving letter Maria von Platen wrote to her friend the critic Oscar Levertin on May 31, 1906, following her breakup with Söderberg (a letter Dreyer would have read, as it was reprinted in Sten Rein's book), von Platen talks about how she commenced her affair with Söderberg: "I fell in love with M.B., wrote to the author whom I didn't know at that point and had never met, told him that it would make me very happy if he at some point wished to drop me a line or two. And thus it became many lines, eventually without sense or reason."[4] By "M.B." she means Martin Birck, the hero of Söderberg's first great autobiographical novel, *Martin Birck's Youth*. If Söderberg was to turn von Platen into a fictional character to make sense of her, von Platen herself had already, even before she met him, fallen in love with Söderberg through the sense she had made of his fictional alter ego. And when his writing turned from "a line or two" into "many lines," it may have precipitated their love affair, but is also became text "without sense or reason." Summing up this emotional journey (mediated through Söderberg's words) that brought her into her relationship with Söderberg, von Platen adds: "But now when I look back, it was like being seated on a bridal chair, blindfolded [att gå i brudstol med förbundna ögon]."[5] As a bride, blinded by words—by the very words that bind her to their

---

3 Von Platen continues to resonate in Scandinavian literary and social history as a woman who embodied a kind of "free will"; a recent biography of her by Kurt Mälarstedt is entitled *Ett liv på egna villkor* (Stockholm: Wallström & Widstrand, 2006), which can be translated "A Life on Her Own Terms."

4 Rein, *Hjalmar Soderbergs Gertrud*, 283. Translation provided by Amanda Doxtater.

5 Ibid.

author—von Platen is at once attached to her man by the sense those words make (firstly, and primarily, as fictions) and then by the nonsense they make (of life itself.) "Tear up my letter into a thousand pieces. Promise, promise me that," von Platen implores near the end of her letter. But of course Levertin didn't, and Dreyer nearly sixty years later was able to avail himself of von Platen's words to fashion his real-and-fictional Gertrud with the help of them, and in many of the same ways to confront the sense and nonsense his sources made of themselves through their words.

After Gertrud and Nygren's discussion of free will, Dreyer follows with Nygren's account of his stay in Paris, where, like Freud, he went to study psychiatry (it is "even more in fashion" than psychology, Nygren tells Gertrud). While there, Nygren and his colleagues hypnotized each other and experimented with telepathy: "We found a woman with a sixth sense; she was quite useful to us."

Why has Dreyer taken so much care to add this almost non-sequitur dialogue here? And who was this woman, and how was she useful to Nygren, and of interest to us? The conjunction of turn-of-the-century Paris, psychiatry, hypnotism, free will, and women creates a very specific matrix, one that Dreyer was focused on for nearly his entire working life. We shall call that matrix "hysteria," and, in the pages to come, we shall understand just how "hysterical" Gertrud's parlor performance really was. For Dreyer himself had spent a good amount of time in Paris with a woman we will show was one of the greatest hysterics ever, a woman with a sixth sense who was quite useful to him, too: Joan of Arc. Joan is, as we shall now see, an exemplary precursor, a kind of Old Testament "type" of Gertrud, and Dreyer's description of her martyrdom was, I think, very present to him as he crafted the scene of Gertrud before the tapestry.

HOW IS *GERTRUD* A KIND OF REMAKE OF *THE PASSION OF JOAN OF ARC*?

To fully understand just how present Joan was to Dreyer in *Gertrud*, we must take an extended detour back to Dreyer's classic film of 1928, *The Passion of Joan of Arc*, a film whose iconography is intimately linked to Nygren's activities in Paris and his devotion to Gertrud. Because Gertrud's struggle to fix her own *istoria* in the images around her—or, rather, her eventual refusal of that goal, and insistence on the sublime failure of that struggle—was precisely the drama being played out during the birth of psychiatry in Paris at which Nygren attended, and its roots were explored with ferocious vision by Dreyer in *Joan*.

We shall understand that vision by exploring, again, the archaeology of another single moment in Dreyer's work. And this moment, too, is all about a violent and obscene conjoining of text and image. That moment comes early in *Joan*, in the midst of her trial, when Jean d'Estivet, easily one of the most repulsive of Joan's accusers—and, as a group, they are a distinctly ugly lot—gets out of his seat, enraged by Joan, and walks out of his shot, to enter, a couple of seconds later, into Joan's. The *Avant-Scène cinéma* decoupage of the sequence describes what follows:

In the left foreground, Joan's face, fixedly gazing heavenwards. From the right of the frame enters d'Estivet, disfigured by anger. He approaches Joan and yells down at her. . . . Joan doesn't react to d'Estivet, whose screaming mouth is nearly glued to her ear. He continues to scream, ending his vociferations by spitting on Joan's face. Joan hardly reacts; she holds her faraway gaze.[1]

1 "La Passion de Jeanne d'Arc," Special issue of *Avant-Scène du Cinéma*, 367–368 (1988): 57. Author's translation. In the published screenplay of *Joan*, we are told that "on Joan's face there lingers the expression of one who is far removed from this world." Carl Theodor Dreyer, *Four*

65

HOW IS GERTRUD A KIND OF REMAKE OF THE PASSION OF JOAN OF ARC?

Let us hold this image, and its description, close at hand: the mouth "nearly glued" to the ear; the ejaculatory speech; the faraway gaze; the spittle that just misses Joan's ear; the shock of d'Estivet's entrance into Joan's close-up space (figs. 10 and 11). It is a violent moment—about as violent as any in the film—and its almost pornographic, insistent theatricality, the emphatic close-up-ness with which it pictures d'Estivet's nastiness, can serve us as an emblem of the entire film's own particular readability, the way *The Passion of Joan of Arc* makes, under a certain kind of duress, sense,[2] a sense intimately linked to the "sixth sense" *Gertrud*'s Nygren so fervently desires access to.

The violence of this moment with d'Estivet is also a function of what we might call its attempt to depict "forced audition." And since *Joan* is a film in which the majority of the action is taken up with the production and reception of human speech (a central fixation of *Gertrud*, too), we should pay particular attention when the relationship between those two activities is called into question and refigured, as it is here, as an exercise of power. In many ways, the film's very coherence is staked on that relation—more than 95 percent of the film's intertitles are, for example, dialogue cards. Hearing, unlike vision, is hard to self-regulate—we can close our eyes to keep a particular sight out, as the woman in the tapestry does, but it is almost impossible to close our ears to keep out an unwanted noise, especially if that noise is the speech of someone just inches away. Dreyer depicts Joan in the seemingly impossible act of "not hearing," and he does so by guiding us toward not her ears but her eyes. Her otherworldly look, so infuriating to d'Estivet, is a sign of her transport away from the violent rhetoric of her accusers into a type of vision that has a very interesting rhetorical history, a vision very much akin to that of Maria von Platen's "blind" bride.

Joan, like the trial on whose transcripts its screenplay is based, is a product of

---

Screenplays, trans. Oliver Stallybrass (Bloomington: Indiana University Press, 1970), 35. This descriptive emphasis on the otherworldly gaze inscribes onto Joan's face a key formal strategy of the film, the refusal to "match" eye-lines, to "follow" the gaze from one shot to the next. I will discuss the significance of this inscription later in this chapter.

2   Linda Williams's now-classic account of the "money shot" in *Hard Core: Power, Pleasure, and the "Frenzy of the Visible"* (Berkeley: University of California Press, 1999) explores the power dynamics at work in this "making visible" of male ejaculate.

66

HOW IS GERTRUD A KIND OF REMAKE OF THE PASSION OF JOAN OF ARC?

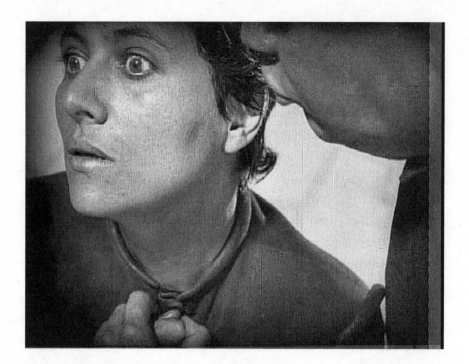

10 Loyseleur breaches the frame. Carl Theodor Dreyer, frame still from *The Passion of Joan of Arc*, Société générale des films, 1928. Film still reprinted from *La passion de Jeanne d'Arc*, a film by Carl Theodor Dreyer © 1928 by Gaumont.

a social practice of meaning-making, and to understand its meanings requires an analysis of how its form is also a kind of function. And it is, also like Joan's trial, a uniquely pressured and contested scene of meaning production, where the infliction of sensation and the making of sense go hand in hand, much the way, at the film's crisis-point, Loyseleur's hand descends onto Joan's in order to guide her signature on her (false) confession.

This hand-in-handness of sense and sensation, of, at its most brutal moments, writing and body, puts into operation a dynamic well known to readers of feminist and psychoanalytic theory, that of the opposition between a Symbolic order often understood as gendered masculine and an Imaginary, "semiotic" image/body continuum gendered feminine. In this dyad, the feminine figures as both a site of resistance to the male symbolic order as well as, paradoxically, its ground.

67

HOW IS GERTRUD A KIND OF REMAKE OF THE PASSION OF JOAN OF ARC?

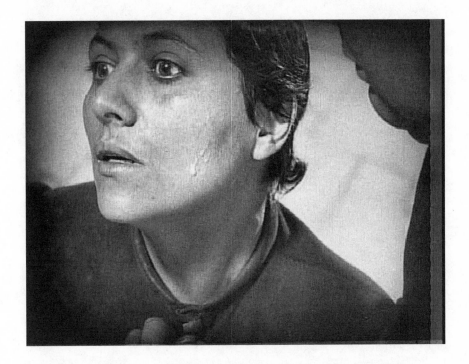

11 Failure to communicate: Loyseleur's missed *conceptio per aurem*. Carl Theodor Dreyer, frame still from *The Passion of Joan of Arc*, Société générale des films, 1928. Film still reprinted from *La passion de Jeanne d'Arc*, a film by Carl Theodor Dreyer © 1928 by Gaumont.

It is easy to read Dreyer's films as both instances and allegories of the battle between a repressed feminine semiotic and an oppressive masculine symbolic regime — but the ease with which such readings can be performed doesn't make them any the less pertinent. I am more interested in giving a history to such "readings" (the term itself bears the marks of its own logocentric assumptions), to show how when confronted with images that bear meaning, criticism itself turns to gender to account for their fecundity. If images signify too, then, to the extent to which we can say they mean something, they tend to take on the properties we associate with the symbolic order — they tend to act like writing, especially to those of us whose job it is to write about them.

The violence of this process of inscribing meaning into and extracting meaning out of the image — critical as it may be — makes up a large part of the texture of *Gertrud* and *The Passion of Joan of Arc*. The cruelty of Dreyer's cinema

68

HOW IS GERTRUD A KIND OF REMAKE OF THE PASSION OF JOAN OF ARC?

and of the narratives it tells is partially a function of the emphasis Dreyer places on the conjunction of meanings and bodies. Images of hands, mouths, ears, and eyes—all of them in *Joan* appear to carry enormous narrative and symbolic weight. But for all their tumescence, they also appear as futile overcompensations for their obvious dysfunctionality—d'Estivet's mouth, for example, is obviously *not* getting through to Joan's ear; the huge eyes we so insistently follow in the film from one shot to the next almost *never* "match." Likewise, in *Gertrud*, Dreyer was fascinated, he said, by the way in which Söderberg's characters talked "past" each other, their words never connecting, no matter how "heavy" Dreyer made them. Indeed, in *Gertrud*, almost no one ever actually looks directly at anyone else—one of the few times this happens is when Gertrud and Nygren look at each other in front of the tapestry, and the only really consistent crosscutting in *Gertrud* occurs at the end of the film, when Gertrud and Nygren part forever. Dreyer uses the cinematic language of connection to underscore the ultimate disconnection Gertrud seeks from the bonds of articulation.

In *Joan*, d'Estivet's screaming mouth at Joan's ear—and Joan's deflected glance, signifying in the register of the visual her refusal to hear—is as strong an image as any of the sheer oppressive political muscle it takes to even begin to get a point across in Dreyer's films. We do not, however, have to judge Dreyer's cinema on some scale of political correctness—we can value it for the instructional pain it inflicts on us as much as we can devalue it for its sadism; and we can applaud it for the potentially liberatory masochistic pleasures it affords while also condemning it for its repetitive, authoritarian style—any of these readings are possible, and it is their mutual coexistence that makes Dreyer's texts so interesting.[3] The grounds for these possible readings, the marks on the face of *Joan*'s and *Gertrud*'s texts that proclaim their readability, are what I shall now proceed to give at least a partial history to.

---

3   The allusion here is to Carol Clover's *Men, Women, and Chain Saws: Gender in the Modern Horror Film* (Princeton: Princeton University Press, 1993), a more than seminal text for what is to follow.

HOW DID THE VIRGIN MARY REALLY GET PREGNANT

(AND IS THAT WHY GERTRUD IS CHILDLESS)?

As a preliminary to such a history, I want to sketch out some visual echoes, perhaps even quotations, that resonate out of that scene with d'Estivet at Joan's ear. As an image that graphically stages the violent encounter between woman and word, it partakes of a long recorded visual history of similar moments that freeze on images of men at women's ears. How these images inscribe or are inscripted into the labor history of the production of their meanings will be our topic for the next few pages, as we turn our gaze away from Dreyer's films and into their prehistory; for d'Estivet's mouth at Joan's ear, attempting a forced entry of language into the body of Dreyer's heroine, takes up a position, however buffoonish and fleshy, occupied by a central player in one of the most persistently pictured scenes in Christian art, of the East as well as of the West—the Annunciation.

The Annunciation is the moment described in Luke and in some important Apocryphal texts when the angel Gabriel announces to the Virgin Mary that she shall conceive and bear the son of God. The encounter is described thus in Luke:

And the Angel came in unto her, and said, Hail, thou that art highly favoured, the Lord is with thee: blessed art thou among women. And when she saw him, she was troubled at his saying, and cast in her mind what manner of salutation this should be. And the angel said unto her, Fear not, Mary: for thou hast found favor with God. And behold, thou shalt conceive in thy womb, and bring forth a son, and shalt call his name Jesus. . . . Then said Mary unto the angel, How shall this be, seeing I know not a man? And the Angel answered and said unto her, The Holy Ghost shall come upon thee, and the power of the highest shall overshadow thee: therefore also the holy thing which shall be born of thee shall be called the son of God. . . . And Mary said, Behold the handmaid of the Lord; be it unto me according to thy word."[1]

The narrative in Luke emphasizes Mary's initial fear and surprise, her inquisitiveness and thoughtfulness, and finally her humility. The pictured versions of the scene have at various times highlighted one or the other of these responses, although they often tend toward the more dramatic, centering on the initial appearance and salutation of the Angel, accompanied by Mary's surprised recoil. Gabriel is usually seen raising his right hand in speech, and in many cases the text of his salutation can be read on a banderole that unfolds from his hand.

In early illuminated manuscript versions of the Annunciation, such as the Rabula Gospels, Gabriel and Mary stand on opposite sides of the written text — the words we read are literally moving from his side to hers. In church decoration, too, the separation of the angel and Mary was part of the figuring of the narrative of the Annunciation. In the Palatine Chapel at Palermo, for example, the two figures stand on either side of the opening of an arch, so that, in the words of Gertrud Schiller, "the actual space between them is, as it were, filled with the angel's message."[2] The two figures show up this way in Giotto's Arena Chapel, on either side of the triumphal arch, and in many churches "it is not uncommon to find the angel and the Virgin each occupying a separate bay in a double arcade."[3] In the Eastern Orthodox churches, Mary and Gabriel appear on the two wings of the main doors of the iconostasis, the screen that divides the sanctuary from the rest of the church.

Let us underscore this spatial separateness. Even when the scene of the Annunciation is represented within the same frame, strong markers of sepa-

---

1   Luke 1:28–38. Revised Standard Version.

2   Gertrud Schiller, *Iconography of Christian Art*, trans. Janet Seligman (Greenwich: New York Graphic Society, 1971), 43.

3   David M. Robb, "The Iconography of the Annunciation in the Fourteenth and Fifteenth Centuries," *Art Bulletin* 18 (1936): 486.

ration are made. As Louis Réau remarks, this is because of the dissymmetry of the heavenly world of Gabriel and earthly realm of Mary. "The consequence" of this dissymmetry, notes Réau, "from the spatial point of view is that the space is fractioned into two unequal and dissimilar parts: instead of a homogenous space, of a simple exterior or interior, we have a mixed space, at once open and closed, with an outside and an inside."[4] This is why so many Annunciations take place in transitional spaces — in loggias, porticos, archways; at windows and doorways; on the borders of enclosed gardens.

Many of these bordered, enclosed spaces also function as symbols of Mary's inviolate — yet violated — womb. As Carol Purtle says of Jan Van Eyck's depiction: "It is clear that both the foreground and background spaces of the Ghent Annunciation were constructed as symbols of the Virgin's womb."[5] Mary's bed chamber, also a symbol of her womb, the *thalamus Virginis*, is often conflated with the interior space of the Church.[6] Perhaps the most ubiquitous symbol of Mary's perpetual virginity is the *hortus conclusus*, or enclosed garden, in which so many Annunciations are placed.

This fractioned, hybrid, unequal space is an inherent part of the drama of the scene, and it gives the Annunciation a kind of internal representational instability that makes it such a modern-seeming tradition. What links these two spaces is, of course, the Annunciation itself; in picturing that moment of speech and of audition, the Annunciation marks off two separate spaces while at the same time conjoining them, in the way that the writing inscribed within the frame conjoins speech and image.

When Dreyer speaks of putting *Gertrud*'s text into the "foreground," and as he proceeds continuously to depict in *Gertrud* hybrid, framed, and multiply bordered spaces in which to place that text, he follows a pictorial strategy refined over centuries of the development of this annunciatory dynamic; *Gertrud*'s form and content are not incidental to each other — they are func-

4   Louis Réau, *Iconographie de l'art Chretien* (Paris: Presses Universitaires de France, 1957), 1:11.

5   Carol J. Purtle, *The Marian Paintings of Jan van Eyck* (Princeton: Princeton University Press, 1982), 32.

6   Robb, "Iconography of the Annunciation," 495.

tions of a powerful ongoing anxiety in Western pictorial culture about the place of the word in the image, and of the role of women in the reception (or, in Dreyer's radical case, the rejection) of that word. To understand just how boldly Dreyer's Gertrud figures within and apart from this tradition, we need to explore further its annunciatory obsessions with its own textuality; indeed, what we described as the "ekphrastic" quality of Dreyer's film is intricately bound up with the gender dynamics of the story the Annunciation's unfolding iconographies tell.

The place of writing, both as a thematic and a formal presence, always played a prominent role in the Annunciation, and the evolving iconography of the scene reflects an ever-increasing awareness of the relation between textuality as such and a textuality organized as a kind of writing. Many early depictions of the Annunciation, for example, relied on a number of apocryphal texts— marginal, anecdotal, later seen as illegitimate—in which Mary was described as receiving the angel while spinning a cloth for the temple. By the late Middle Ages Mary's spindle was replaced by a book, and instead of interrupting her weaving, her text-making, the angel is seen disturbing her reading (fig. 12). Mostly, Mary reads from the Old Testament, from Isaiah, the prophecy which begins, "Behold, a virgin shall conceive."[7] And the reading desk on which Mary's Bible is placed is often made the marker of the border between Mary's space and Gabriel's. Here, the old word provides a border that the new word crosses: language is itself a liminal space.[8]

The lectern, and the book atop it, replace the earlier, more architectural barriers between Mary and Gabriel while still "acknowledging the traditional dichotomy"[9] between them, representing a kind of interiorization of the more

7   Isaiah 7:14. Revised Standard Version.

8   The power of the new word to supersede the old is emphasized in Leonardo's Uffizi Annunciation, in which "the letters on Mary's Bible appear to be legible yet make no real sense." Paul J. Cardile, "Observations on the Iconography of Leonardo da Vinci's Uffizi Annunciation," *Studies in Iconography* 7, no. 8 (1981–82): 194. The new word has turned the old words into mere images of themselves.

9   Robb, "Iconography of the Annunciation," 488.

12 **The Word as barrier and medium. Leonardo da Vinci, *Annunciation*, Galleria degli Uffizi, Florence. Reprinted by permission from Scala, Art Resource, New York.**

emphatically marked hybrid spaces of earlier Annunciations. More and more, writing takes the "place" of architecture, as the angel and Mary begin to be positioned in more intimate, less cordoned off, relations. Two Annunciations by Botticelli tell this story well; in his earlier rendition (fig. 13), the book and lectern add to the architectural barriers placed between Mary and Gabriel. Four years later, Botticelli would move the book to one side and place the two figures in close proximity in a single space (fig. 14). Gabriel's exteriority is made merely coincidental by framing him in front of a doorway giving a view to the outside.

This progressive movement toward "spatial unity" in the picturings of the Annunciation was pointed out by David Robb, in an influential 1936 account of the iconography of the scene. For Robb, the bringing together of the angel and Mary was simply the attainment, over time, of a correct and proper depiction of architecturally and perspectivally unified space. "Duccio," for example, "did not succeed in attaining complete spatial unity," while Pucelle attempted "a compromise between exterior and interior elements in the setting," and

13 Hybrid space: The Annunciation. Sandro Botticelli, *The Annunciation*, Metropolitan Museum of Art, New York. Reprinted by permission from the Metropolitan Museum of Art, New York.

another work from the Pucelle workshop must have been made by the hand of an inferior assistant, as it was done "without much understanding (the architecture shows an even greater confusion of interior and exterior elements)."[10] We may argue with Robb's rather limited empathy for earlier, less "correct" representations of the Annunciation, but Robb does rightly emphasize the strength of a tradition that simultaneously erects clearly demarcated separate spaces while confusing and questioning the very distinction between exterior and interior itself.[11] Mary Ann Caws, understanding this questioning of borders as

10 Ibid., 493–94.

11 John R. Spencer gives a more up-to-date and highly nuanced account of the changes in the "spatial imagery" of Florentine Annunciations, noting a "compromise solution" in Fra Filippo

14 "Do not fall into these errors": The Annunciation. Sandro Botticelli, *The Annunciation*, Galleria degli Uffizi, Florence, Italy. Reprinted by permission from Alinari, Art Resource, New York.

the central subject of the scene, has even suggested that one might categorize Annunciations "by the sort of separating device, and the effect of the separation upon the scene, and the agent and manner of penetration through that

Lippi's San Lorenzo altarpiece, in which "the architecture no longer encloses the action, but serves as a screen separating the space of the painting from the space of the beholder" (278). Spencer, "Spatian Imagery of the Annunciation in Fifteenth Century Florence," *The Art Bulletin* 37 (1955): 273–80.

separating device."[12] Recognizing a "veiled erotic charge" in the infringement of the barrier that separates Mary and the angel, she notes the importance of the countervailing forces of resistance and separation.[13] And that erotic charge is intimately linked to the function of language and the speech that carries it across spatial, and temporal, barriers.

But why this insistence on language and its function in the Annunciation? On language as both that which separates and brings together the heavenly and the earthly? One reason is that the Annunciation is not merely the moment when Mary is told she will conceive, it is also, according to Church dogma, the *moment of conception itself*. Here, for example, is a passage from the Eastern church liturgy for the Feast of the Annunciation: "As she heard the words of the archangel so she received in a supernatural manner in her undefiled womb the son and the word of god, his wisdom."[14] The Annunciation is not just the picturing of a moment of speech and hearing, it is also the picturing of the moment when God's Word—the Logos—enters the world and conceives. To put it crudely, what Mary hears is what she gets.

And so the notion of *conceptio per aurem*, "conception through the ear," so central to Catholic accounts of the Virgin conception. As a thirteenth-century English dancing song put it:

Glad us maiden, mother mild
Through thine ear thou were with child
Gabriel he said it thee . . .[15]

The idea of conception through the ear had some interesting consequences for the picturing of the scene, as theologians began to relate Psalm 45 ("Hearken, o daughter, and incline thine ear") as an injunction applied to the Annun-

---

12 Mary Ann Caws, "The Annunciation of a Text: Rilke and the Birth of the Poem," *The Eye in the Text* (Princeton: Princeton University Press, 1981), 110.

13 Ibid., 109.

14 Schiller, *Iconography of Christian Art*, 43.

15 Schiller, *Iconography of Christian Art*, 43.

ciation, which, in Schiller's words, "caused artists to depict Mary with her head inclined to one side in a pose which appears frequently from the eleventh century onwards."[16] In the thirteenth century, under the influence of Franciscan theology, which stressed the active role of the Trinity in the Annunciation, we start to see an emphasis on (in Luke's words) God's "overshadowing" of Mary, usually in the form of the dove descending to her ear; and many times the Christ child is seen descending on a ray of light, often holding a cross that prefigures his later sacrifice. In the Lady Chapel of the fifteenth-century cathedral at Wurzburg, the whole story is almost comically made manifest: God the father, up in heaven, holds in his mouth a tube which carries his word to Mary's ear, upon which the dove stands, while the Christ child is depicted as sliding down the tube.

The theory of the *conceptio per aurem* also helps us to understand Mary's surprise and fear; by the time of the Renaissance, the sexual charge of the scene was becoming pretty manifest. As Johannes Tauer, a pupil of Eckhart's, described the scene, "Mary was troubled because of the majesty of that salutation and also because of the state of ravishment in which she was discovered."[17] Many artists, such as Botticelli, showed a dangerous predilection for emphasizing the early stages of Mary's response, her fear and surprise, which by Botticelli's day was coded openly as having a sexual charge. Other artists committed themselves with gusto to the opportunities the scene offered for depicting violent action. Leonardo da Vinci, for one, did not approve of these renderings: "[S]ome days ago I saw the picture of an angel who, in making the Annunciation, seemed to be trying to chase Mary out of her room, with movements showing the sort of attack one might make on some hated enemy; and Mary, as if desperate, seemed to be trying to throw herself out of the window. Do not fall into errors like these."[18]

16 Schiller, *Iconography of Christian Art*, 43.

17 Don Denny, *The Annunciation from the Right from Early Christian Times to the Sixteenth Century* (New York: Garland, 1977), 141.

18 Quoted in Michael Baxandall, *Painting and Experience in Fifteenth-Century Italy* (Oxford: Oxford University Press, 1972), 56.

These were, however, errors easy to fall into. As Yrjö Hirn put it in the rather quaint language of 1909: "If we are compelled to disapprove of the too worldly element in the later Renaissance representations of the Annunciation, still we must admit that the scene was often treated, even during the devout Middle Ages, in a way which did not quite harmonize with the strict serious-ness of the mystery. The situation itself, the meeting between the young virgin and the heavenly youth, was such that a deviation from the severe theological interpretation could with difficulty be avoided."[19] It was difficult, Hirn notes, "not to think of Mary as one thinks of an earthly maiden receiving a message from her lover." The problem was that, with the greater realism of the later Renaissance painters, the "message" read more like a rape than a love letter: "Tintoretto paints the extremity of fear in the Virgin. . . . Lorenzo Lotto has made Mary stretch forth her hands in almost petrified terror," and so on.[20]

Because of the all-too-human dramatic possibilities inherent in the Annun-ciation, there was a great effort during the Renaissance to chart and catego-rize, and thus to make theologically intelligible and inoffensive, the different stages of the Annunciation. Michael Baxandall quotes at length from one of the most influential popular preachers of the Italian fifteenth century, Fra Roberto Caracciolo de Lecce. Baxandall shows how popular preaching helped organize the experience of viewing art into manageable units of narrative meaning and gives as an example Fra Roberto's preaching on the mystery of the Angelic Colloquy of the Annunciation, in which the preacher lays out five successive spiritual and mental conditions or states attributable to Mary. Here is a bit of Fra Roberto's account:

19 Yrjo Hirn, *The Sacred Shrine: A Study of the Poetry and Art of the Catholic Church* (Boston, Beacon Press, 1957), 290.

20 Ibid., 291, 289. By the late nineteenth century, the scene of the Annunciation would become both more unified in its spatial presentation and even more sexualized, as the "realism" of the depiction of Mary's impregnation becomes foregrounded. Colin Cruise gives a wonderful account of Pre-Raphaelite uses of the Annunciation in "Versions of the Annunciation: Wilde's Aestheticism and the Message of Beauty," *After the Pre-Raphaelites: Art and Aestheticism in Victorian England*, ed. Elizabeth Prettejohn (Rutgers University Press, 1999), 167–87.

The third mystery of the Annunciation is called Angelic Colloquy; it comprises five laudable Conditions of the Blessed Virgin:

1. Conturbatio—Disquiet
2. Cogitatio—Reflection
3. Interrogatio—Inquiry
4. Humiliatio—Submission
5. Meritatio—Merit.[21]

Fra Roberto then goes on to expound on each of the five stages. Here, for example, is an excerpt from his description of Humiliatio: "What tongue could ever describe, indeed, what mind could contemplate the movement and style with which she set on the ground her holy knees? Lowering her head she spoke: Behold the handmaid of the lord. . . . And then, lifting her eyes to heaven, and bringing up her hands with her arms in the form of a cross, she ended as God, the angels, and the Holy Fathers desired: be it unto me according to thy word."[22]

Mary's speech, the fruition of the desire of the fathers, tells simply of her bearing of the word unto herself, while the raising up of her arms into the shape of a cross figures Mary's fulfillment of that desire as her own Passion. Her upraised arms are mirrored in the uplifting of her gaze, for the bearing of the word causes also a Passion in the register of the visual. In her final station, the Meritatio, this Passion resolves into a vision split between body and heaven: "So we can justly suppose that in the moment when the Virgin Mary conceived Christ her soul rose to such lofty and sublime contemplation of the action and sweetness of divine things that, in the presence of the beatific vision, she passed beyond the experience of every other created being. . . . Probably, in her profound humility, she raised her eyes to heaven and then lowered them

---

21 Another contemporary account divided the Annunciation into three separate moments, and recent scholars have argued for anywhere from two to seven. See Cardile, "Observations on the Iconography," 189.

22 Baxandall, *Painting and Experience*, 54.

80

HOW DID THE VIRGIN MARY REALLY GET PREGNANT (AND IS THAT WHY GERTRUD IS CHILDLESS)?

towards her womb with many tears, saying something like: 'Who am I, that have conceived God incarnate.'"[23]

Keeping in mind these poses, these tears, these ecstatic outstretched arms, these fulfillments of divine desires, as well as the movements of Mary's gaze, from womb to heaven and back to womb, we can begin to see, at the level of acting style alone, how the portrayal of Joan in *The Passion of Joan of Arc* marks her as following in the visual tradition of the Annunciation as it has been worked out in elaborate iconographical and narratological detail over the centuries.

And let us not forget the woman in *Gertrud's* tapestry, either. Her strange calm; her hidden, though lowered, gaze; her arms, seemingly descending from the shape of a crucifix; and the erotic charge of the hounds' attack on her naked body, a long-established metaphor for sexual ravishment—all these remind us of the final stage of the Virgin's Merit. They should also bring to mind the full, violent weight behind the metaphor of Lessing's "pregnant moment," that moment where story, fully "conceived" and already articulated, is just shy of imaging its climax.

For the connection is stronger still. The Annunciation, in the totality of all its picturings, is a prototypical staging of the encounter between text and image, of the intersection of word and woman—the moment when the Logos is both spoken to and enters into the Virgin body of its material support (from the Latin *mater*, "mother"). As Julia Kristeva might describe it, here is the scene where the symbolic meets and transforms the semiotic. The sexual charge, the pictorial and spatial instability, the hybrid mapping of interiority and exteriority, the mise-en-scène of feminine fear and humility, the use of the book and of language as both border and breakthrough, the representational challenge of picturing speech and hearing—all of these function within a long tradition that sees the marriage of signifier and signified as anything but a love match. The word, in order to be heard by men, must be materialized, and if the woman gets to traffic with heaven in ways unavailable to men, it is only because her body is placed at the disposal of a male economy of signification. The anxiety as to

23 Ibid., 55.

whether the female body "tells" everything it "hears," as to whether it properly translates the word into the world, produces such powerfully resonant and productive moments as that of the Annunciation. But the impregnating word, as it is made flesh, also carries the risk that it can miscarry, as a more recent stage in the history of that scene will show us.[24]

24 Michael Ann Holly, in a wonderful chapter in *Past Looking: Historical Imagination and the Rhetoric of the Image* (Ithaca: Cornell University Press, 1996) entitled "Witnessing an Annunciation," uses Robert Campin's depiction of the Annunciation in his Merode Alterpiece (ca. 1425) to critique the methodologies of modern art history, in particular Panofsky's Iconology. "Campin's work of art is, on the one hand, about barriers and, on the other, about the process of getting through them" (158). She argues that the "spectatorial exchange" between "the visual rhetoric of the image and the rhetorical and textual strategies of its historical interpreters" can cross those barriers if we resist Panofsky's reduction of the meaning of an image to the "texts or systems of textuality that precede and thereby absorb the images" (162). My reading here is meant to give a history to one particular aspect of that resistance.

WHY ARE JOAN AND GERTRUD SO "HYSTERICAL"?

The phrase "the word made flesh," was first applied to the study of Dreyer's films by Mark Nash, in an essay on what he identified as the "hysterical" qualities of Dreyer's film texts. For the word made flesh is, of course, also the formula for conversion hysteria, the construction of a paradigmatically female body whose symptoms, as Freud argued, "speak" the repressed contents of the unconscious. Before taking up the issue of the "hysteria" of Dreyer's films, though, let us take a look at how the theatrical staging of the female hysterical body relates to the iconographical history I've just delivered—and to the conversation Nygren and Gertrud have in front of the tapestry about his psychiatric studies in Paris. For the iconography of the hysterical attack, as it was choreographed and analyzed by early modern psychiatry, bears a striking resemblance to the iconography of the Annunciation. In fact, hysteria (the word comes from the Greek word *hysteron*, "womb"—hysteria thus being the disease of the wandering or dysfunctional womb) is, in its performance, a perfect parody of the Virgin's conception of Christ. And the categorization of the Virgin Mary's "laudable conditions" or positions in the Annunciation, and early psychiatry's categorization of the phases of hysterical attack, are amazingly identical. My claim is that hysterical pregnancy is thus a miscarriage of the Word; the diagnostic grids that read the image of the woman's body for symptoms of her displaced symbolic maternity perform the same attempt at the textual control over the errant female body that the theology of Gabriel's announcement attempts.

The images of this theater of hysteria come from the last part of the nineteenth century, from the by now somewhat familiar photographic records of La Salpetrière, the vast hospital complex in Paris, which, at its heyday, housed more than four thousand women. Freud went there in the 1880s to study under its renowned leader, Jean-Martin Charcot, whose Tuesday afternoon lecture/demonstrations at the Salpetrière amphitheater, the famous *Leçons du Mardi*, were attended by many of the leading Parisian intellectuals of the day. During these sessions Charcot would bring out his hysterical patients, and, inducing hysterical attacks by any number of means (often by hypnotizing them, or by pressing down upon, not uncoincidentally, the ovarian region), he would lecture while the patients performed their symptoms. It is precisely these kinds of demonstrations in Paris that Gertrud's friend Axel Nygren referred to in front of the tapestry.

Charcot was constantly trying to categorize the various phases of the hysterical attack and label them; his labels changed continuously, and he always held that the different phases didn't necessarily succeed one another in a regular order, but he still kept up a constant effort of discrimination.[1]

Sometimes there were four phases: an onset; an "aura hysterica," which was a kind of nimbus of anxiety; an epileptic phase ("now the real drama begins!" Charcot would shout to his audience); and a final, semi- or unconscious phase called "clonic."[2] Or the four phases went like this: an epileptoid phase (Charcot's hysterics acted much like epileptics, probably because after he took over La Salpetrière he decided to house the hysterics in the same ward as the epileptics[3]); a phase of "large movements," of "attitudes" or poses called "passionelles" (fig. 15); hallucinations; and finally deliria.[4] The archetype of the phases of attack was probably three-fold: epileptoid; exotic movements; hallucination.[5]

I think the general pattern, as well as its affinities with the stages of the Annunciation, is clear. An initial moment of fearful recoil, a series of poses and gestures (many of them, here, simply parodies of the poses of sexual

1   See Jean-Martin Charcot, *Lectures on the Diseases of the Nervous System*, trans. George Sigerson (Philadelphia: Henry C. Lea, 1879), 252ff.

2   Charcot, *Leçons du Mardi a la Salpetriere: Policliniques 1887–1888. Notes de cours de MM. Blin, Charcot, et Colin* (Paris: M. Delahaye et Emile Lecrosnier, 1887), 251.

3   Charcot, *Charcot the Clinician: The Tuesday Lessons*, trans. Christopher G. Goetz (New York: Raven Press, 1987), 112.

4   Charcot, *Leçons*, 203. This was Freud's and Breuer's understanding of the "grande crise hysterique." Sigmund Freud and Joseph Breuer, *Studies on Hysteria*, trans. James Strachey and Alix Strachey (New York: Penguin, 1974), 13.

5   Charcot, *Charcot the Clinician*, 104.

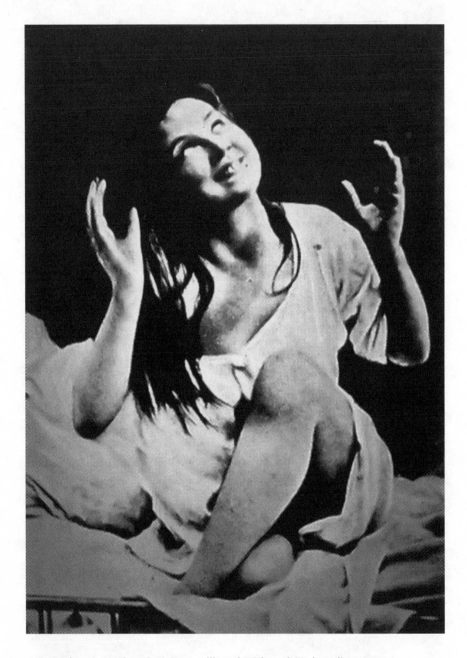

15 Hysteric as Annunciate. D. M. Bourneville and P. Régnard, "Debute d'une Attaque Planche XXVIII," *Photographic Iconography of Salpêtrière*, Library of Congress Online Catalogue for *Freud: Conflict & Culture*. Reprinted from D. M. Bourneville and P. Régnard, *Photographic Iconography of Salpêtrière*, 3 vols. (Paris: Progres Medical, 1876–1880).

intercourse and of birthing), and, finally, the beatific access to other worlds, the hallucinatory stage. From Conturbatio through Humiliatio and finally to Meritatio, the hysteric parodically follows the course of the Virgin's pregnancy, placing herself in a diagnostic grid of highly symbolic poses—poses elaborated and modified over centuries of visual culture. In the theatrical space of the medical interrogation, the hysterical body thus became "readable" as a field of symptoms.

To remark solely the similarity of poses, though, is to go not far enough in interrogating the deep structures, the shared narrative, of the Annunciation and the hysterical attack. For from the earliest accounts on, hysteria has always been closely linked to language and to troubles with the symbolic order. Its first mention, in the oldest medical papyrus preserved from ancient Egypt, calls for the genitals of the hysterical woman to be fumigated either with the fumes from male excrement or from a wax ibis—a symbol of the god Toth, the inventor of writing and the scribe to the gods. By the early seventeenth century Edward Jordan could write a pamphlet entitled *A Briefe Discourse of the Disease Called the Suffocation of the Mother*, it being called so because "most commonly it take them with chocking in the throat."[6] This *furor uterinus*, the wandering of the womb until it keeps the woman from proper speech, clearly resonates in Freud's early, pioneering accounts of hysteria. Katharina, for example, one of Freud and Joseph Breuer's "studies in hysteria," makes a typical complaint: "I get so out of breath. Not always. But sometimes it catches me so that I think I shall suffocate."[7] Hysteria is an interference by the organs of reproduction with the work of symbolic production, rendering them both impotent.

Hysterics, Freud claimed, were visual, not verbal types. (As Joan Copjec notes, Freud uncannily described Charcot in precisely the same terms, as a "seer."[8]) And the cure, first worked out by Anna O. in her sessions with Freud's colleague, Breuer, was, of course, the "talking cure," the replacement of the

6   Ilza Veith, *Hysteria: The History of a Disease* (Chicago: University of Chicago Press, 1965), 125.

7   Ibid.

8   Joan Copjec, "Flavit et Dissipati Sunt," in *October: The First Decade, 1976–1986*, ed. Annette Michelsen et al. (Cambridge: MIT Press, 1987), 296–316.

symptom/pictures with verbal texts.[9] Conversion hysteria was the conversion of language into pictures, into symptoms readable on the body, and as such it was a parodic version of Christ's conception, a monstrous virgin birth. The goal of the talking cure was to reconvert the pictures back into language.

When reading today the transcripts of some of Charcot's sessions, many of which Freud attended, one cannot help but be struck by the recurring issue of what kind of "sense" the hysterical women made to the gathered audience. Immediately following the compression of one young woman's ovarian region, for example, came this dialogue:

Patient: Mother, I am frightened!

Charcot: Note the emotional outburst.

Later, she cries again: Oh! Mother!

Charcot: Again, note these screams. You could say it is a lot of noise over nothing.
     True epilepsy is much more serious and also much more quiet.[10]

The hysterical body is a body that can only make sense as a medium of meaning, as a site for its placement, but not for its production. A common feature of modern hysteria is crucial in this context: the pervasive anesthesia, the literal "insensibility," of the hysterical body, as if it were a body that could "make sense" only for its readers, not for itself. This body, though, could still "remember" the writing it could not itself author or consciously understand. In what we might call the "Jeanne d'Arc" experiment, Charcot would place a long pen in the anesthetic hand of a hysteric, and, while she was looking away, would write out the name "Jean"—the masculine of Jeanne. The hysteric was then asked to repeat the signature, and, to the delight of the doctors, was able to do so perfectly.[11] Like the woman in *Gertrud*'s tapestry, the hysteric's averted gaze guarantees the authenticity of the text her anesthetic body calmly enacts.

9   See Copjec, "Flavit et Dissipati Sunt," 297ff.

10   Charcot, *Charcot the Clinician*, 102.

11   Pierre Janet recounts this among many of the theatrical performances of Charcot's hysterics. See *Major Symptoms of Hysteria* (New York: Macmillan, 1920). For a masterful introduction to Charcot, see Georges Didi-Huberman, *Invention de l'hysterie* (Paris: Macula, 1982).

Gertrud herself, however, refuses to make sense of the texts inscribed in front of and within her; her pain before the tapestry, and subsequent collapse, are marks of the agon between self-authorship and citation she enacts for us.

With this history of gestures and poses present, let us return to the scene in *Joan* with d'Estivet. On a superficial level it is easy to see *Joan* as taking place within a visual culture with a long line of virgins facing texts, ravished by writing. Dreyer's Joan rehearses the iconography, and more fundamentally, the discursive strategies of these earlier stagings of the woman-word encounter, as it both reproduces and makes manifest the sexual politics of its textuality. When d'Estivet loudly (if to us, silently) ejaculates into Joan's ear, he just misses it—and this near-miss is an interesting marker of the way in which Dreyer picks up the master story of the *conceptio per aurem*. The hysteria of Dreyer's text gives birth to a new account of the human subject's relation to the symbolic order.

As Noel Burch has pointed out, *Joan's* key formal strategy is this: "[I]t contains absolutely no 'situation' shots to 'map out' the topology of the main setting (the court-room)."[12] Burch is correct to remind us of this lack of established space. But, in an important way, the film does utilize a manner of "establishing" shots—shots, however, whose adequacy is always under question. For the only shots in the film that Joan and her accusers actually "share" are, as a rule, the intertitles, the dialogue cards of the questions and answers that get tossed back and forth between the judges' and Joan's separate spaces. *Joan of Arc* is a silent film "sutured" not by shot/reverse shots, not by establishing shots and eyeline matches, but by the written traces of the characters' speech. This speech is understood to have the ability to "cross" from shot to shot. It links the film's characters, as they speak and hear, in a shared aural/graphic space.

This border space, made up of words and crossed by words,[13] is precisely the

12 Noel Burch, "Carl Theodor Dreyer: The Major Phase," in *Cinema: A Critical Dictionary*, ed. Richard Roud (New York: Nationwide Book Services, 1980), 1:297.

13 Bordwell gives a detailed and thoughtful analysis of the film as a battle between the written and spoken word. I build here on many of his observations. Bordwell sees the film as "putting into tension the spoken and the written word," pitting Joan's "inspired speech [as] opposed to the ossification of the written record." *Films of Carl-Theodor Dreyer*, 91. The film's images, according to Bordwell, function in "dialogue" with the intertitles, which, as writing, become "only the trace of Jeanne's dynamic speech and necessarily clashes with the very immediacy

space in which Dreyer locates his camera, never establishing a common space for his characters, but always occupying the space their words traverse, a space never the "same," always divided. In *Joan*, Dreyer recreates the scenographics of the *conceptio per aurem*, but he stresses their literal obscenity, they way they create an offstage for each of their participants that the word can never completely conjoin. Dreyer insists on the violence of the sexual dynamics of the word's hybridizing and destabilizing of space as an integral part of his work.

The few times when eye-line matches actually function coherently in *Joan*, and therefore cohere the mixed space of the movie over and through its intertitles, are thematized as moments of profound deception, just as such matches are thematized in *Gertrud* as moments of tragic disconnection. This is most forcefully apparent in the scene where Loyseleur, after having gained Joan's confidence with a forged letter from King Charles, leads her on to more and more damning answers during a subsequent interrogation. The questions are posed, and Joan pauses and looks to Loyseleur, who nods the response, and then Joan gives her answer. It is only near the end of the interrogation that she realizes her mistake in trusting him, when he breaks the most consistently matched sequence of shots in the film.[14]

The lesson for the viewer is clear—we, like Joan, should not be mislead in our reading of the film by "following" the relay of gazes, nor by reading the intertitles as linking their readers in the shared social space of the symbolic order. Our isolation, like Joan's, is made even more acute by the fact that Joan and the judges so rarely appear within the same shot, something that gives the entrance of d'Estivet into the same frame as Joan a particular violence—he destabilizes an already unstable sequence of matches and violates a kind of cinematic *hortus conclusus* that has kept us, with Joan, relatively if only provisionally safe from the encroaching Word.

---

which the speech embodies" (91). He sees the film as "putting into tension the spoken and the written word," pitting Joan's "inspired speech [as] opposed to the ossification of the written record" (91).

14 See Richard Abel, who reads the episode as part of a general movement in the film toward a centralization of subjectivity and organization of space around Joan, in *The French Cinema: The First Wave, 1915–1929* (Princeton: Princeton University Press, 1984), 493.

Freud, who had often compared the symptomatology of hysteria with a "pictographic script," which has become intelligible "after the discovery of a few bilingual inscriptions,"[15] tried determinedly to overturn Charcot's "visual" approach to diagnosis by emphasizing the linguistic translatability of the picture-script presented to him by his hysterical patients.[16] Dreyer, however, insists on holding in dynamic tension the image and the word. The discovery of a few "bilingual inscriptions" gives proof for Freudian analysis of the status of the Virgin's poses as "script," as sign, and thus, even in its most miscarried form, as guarantor of the ultimate triumph of the Word. In Dreyer, however, the Word makes of the image not so much a sign but a mark, a kind of iconoclastic scarring.

It is this dynamic that also helps explain the intensity of the violence of Dreyer's aesthetic. In his early films, Dreyer took the forced submission of a film to its textual authorities to its practical extreme, even making his actors, for example, memorize their lines—not exactly standard procedure in the production of silent films.[17] This is why it was possible, in the awful 1952 reedit of *Joan* by Lo Duca, to substitute a number of intertitles with subtitles: as the actors mouth, in order, the exact words of the trial transcript, we can easily read their lips.[18] On the one hand, Dreyer was attempting to banish the "meaningless obscenities" he saw emerging from the mouths of the actors in his first film; but on the other hand, Dreyer creates a profound and violent mise-en-scène centered on the torture by language of the body into its readable expression. In Dreyer, as in de Sade, this scene of writing the body is the index of a

---

15 Freud and Breuer, *Studies on Hysteria,* 129.

16 For an account of Freud's turn to the linguistic from the visually dominated approach of Charcot, see Martin Jay, *Downcast Eyes: The Denigration of Vision in Twentieth-Century French Thought* (Berkeley: University of California Press, 1993), 357ff.

17 The only silent film in which Dreyer didn't follow this practice, *The Bride of Glomdal* (1926), is also his weakest.

18 *Gertrud,* oddly, is another of Dreyer's films that has suffered post facto from the excision of written texts from its release prints; Dreyer had commissioned a number of verses from Grethe Risbjerg Thomsen that served as interstitial chapter markers, but these were at some later point removed from the film, and current versions of *Gertrud* available on DVD do not include them.

deadly serious anxiety about the adequacy of writing and of representation in general to express the self at its moment of purest consciousness—a consciousness in the realist tradition that is paradoxically an awareness of the self's own textuality. Unlike Gabriel's announcement, the Word in Dreyer never quite hits its mark; and it is just this *failure* that forms the ground for Dreyer's great achievement, not just in *Joan* but in *Gertrud*, too.

We have made a long detour away from, but also into and through, the violent forest Gertrud ponders in the tapestry on the wall behind her. Every detail Dreyer planted to create the moment of her look into and away from that image—everything from Nygren's seemingly inconsequential small talk to Dreyer's rigorous refusal to employ standard eye-line match cuts—all of it implicates a complex and profound history of the picturings of women being impregnated with words. Gertrud's refusal of the marriage of image and text, her willful (or, as Sten Rein put it, her "hysteroid") miscarriage of sense, is the source of her tragic heroism, and of Dreyer's entire approach to *Gertrud*. To understand this particular kind of tragedy is to understand how Dreyer, by rupturing the marriage between word and image, approaches the real.

HOW DOES THE STRUGGLE BETWEEN DREYER'S WORDS AND IMAGES OPEN US UP TO THE REAL?

If in much of the theory and practice of Western textuality language functions in the service of a powerful symbolic order that relentlessly seeks to regenerate and extend its power over and through the material body of its subjects, the reading of the body as a *symbol* of resistance to the symbolic appears to beg the question of just what place the body—and its image—has in this struggle.

Adding to the significance of this paradox is the insistent "gendering" of the issue, which, as we have seen, is formidable, in the Western tradition at least. Feminist theory has crucially remarked upon this engenderment, especially in the wake of psychoanalytic, and particularly Lacanian, theory. The alignment of the "feminine" with the prelinguistic "Imaginary" realm, and of the masculine with the "Symbolic" imposition of "the name of the Father" (the interpellation of the human subject into the order of language) has allowed psychoanalytically inclined critics to uncover a powerful set of dynamics in works such as *Joan* and *Gertrud*. They trace a narrative that depicts how the feminine is both excluded from and imprisoned within the "regime of the symbolic," to paraphrase from Deborah Linderman's careful account of *The Passion of Joan of Arc* in her essay "Uncoded Images in the Heterogeneous Text."[1] In that essay, Linderman argues that *Joan* includes "extra," surplus shots (such as the images near the end of the film of a baby being breastfed by its mother, or of the carnivalesque circus performers) that "signify the impossible position of the feminine in the symbolic order of the patriarchy."[2] These marginal shots,

---

1   Deborah Linderman, "Uncoded Images in the Heterogeneous Text," *Wide Angle* 3, no. 3 (1980): 34–41.

2   Ibid.

92

HOW DOES THE STRUGGLE BETWEEN DREYER'S WORDS AND IMAGES OPEN US UP TO THE REAL?

according to Linderman, interruptive as they are of the "dominant diegesis," and easily "excised from both the narrative track and the image track without damage to the textual system,"[3] function as a kind of subversive index of "the violence suppressed by the textuality of the text."[4]

Linderman sees, by definition, the exclusion of the maternal and the feminine from the symbolic, but at the same time seeks to show that this excluded feminine can appear somehow within or alongside the "textual system" without being a part of it. But just how these *uncoded* images get *coded* as *uncoded*, how it is that they signify their insignificance, is difficult to say if we stick too closely to too straightforward an opposition between Imaginary and Symbolic, feminine and masculine, image and word. Linderman is certainly correct in identifying a violent textuality at work in *The Passion of Joan of Arc*, but perhaps it is precisely this "textual system" that requires the inclusion of the "uncoded" presence of a marginal, seemingly "insignificant" feminine. The presence of images coded "feminine" is therefore not necessarily, in Linderman's words, "the inscription of inadvertent meanings into a text," meanings that "reveal ambivalent intentionality,"[5] but is, perhaps, a necessary and intentional part of Dreyer's text.

Julia Kristeva has herself warned of too insistent a "valorization of difference," as Toril Moi says, in which, as Kristeva puts it, "it is all too easy to pass from the search for *difference* to the denegation of the symbolic. The latter is the same as to remove the 'feminine' from the order of language. . . . In other words, if the feminine *exists*, it only exists in the order of significance or signifying process, and it is only in relation to meaning and signification, positioned as their excessive or transgressive other that it *exists*, *speaks*, *thinks* (itself) and *writes* (itself) for both sexes."[6]

3   Ibid., 35.

4   Ibid., 38.

5   Ibid., 35. In conclusion, Linderman proposes that the "enunciations of his camera may have suggested to Dreyer a doubt of which he was hardly conscious." "Uncoded Images," 41. Linderman is here able to support an idea of ambivalent intentionality only by ascribing such intentionality to Dreyer's camera.

6   Julia Kristeva, *Desire in Language: A Semiotic Approach to Literature and Art*, trans. Thomas Gora, Alice Jardine, and Leon S. Roudiez (New York: Columbia University Press, 1980), 11.

93

HOW DOES THE STRUGGLE BETWEEN DREYER'S WORDS AND IMAGES OPEN US UP TO THE REAL?

Kristeva here wants, reasonably, to have it both ways; on the one hand, the feminine exists only within the order of significance, while on the other hand, it exists only so far as it exceeds or is outside that order. A number of theorists, among them Jacqueline Rose, Theresa de Lauretis, Kaja Silverman, and Gaylyn Studlar, have all contested this murky banishment of the feminine to a realm somehow beyond the borders of the symbolic. Silverman, for example, argues that the pre-Oedipal tableau of maternal plenitude so heavily relied upon by Kristeva is in fact an after-the-fact construction that "permits the subject who has already entered into language and desire to dream of maternal unity and phenomenal plenitude."[7] And this is a just description, in fact, of the project Dreyer's autobiography, as well as his cinema, sets in place.[8]

We have previously noted Dreyer's own "illegitimate" origins, made legible (if not legitimate) to him through the dry documents of the social and legal order that tragically marginalized his mother's life and death.[9]

Dreyer, with a filial compulsion, would picture the writing of those documents again and again in his films. The process of that translation into images — a process that often results in the writing of the woman's death certificate — could be called the "signature" aspect of Dreyer's work.[10] Like the signature, Dreyer's images are both written and graphic, a writing that asserts its identity not through its adherence to the rules of any signifying system but through its authenticity as a mark, as evidence or trace of the presence of a free subject.

This is why the greatest crisis in *Joan* is also perhaps its closest close-up — the moment Joan decides to sign her recantation and so save her life. Illiterate (as she informed her judges at the beginning of the film, she learned her "Our

7   Nancy Frankenberry, review of *Nature's Self: Our Journey from Origin to Spirit,* by Robert S. Corrington, *Journal of the American Academy of Religion* 66, no. 1 (Spring 1998): 173.

8   For de Lauretis, the position of the feminine and of feminine desire within representation is "contradictory—but not impossible." *Alice Doesn't* (Bloomington: Indiana University Press, 1984), 38.

9   Martin Drouzy has collected these often hauntingly moving documents in his *Kildemateriale til en Biografi om Carl Th. Dreyer* (Copenhagen: C. A. Reitzels Forlag, 1982).

10 Uncannily, even Dreyer's adoptive father was a sacrifice of sorts to the Symbolic; he died of poisoning as a result of the inks he was exposed to as a professional typographer.

94

HOW DOES THE STRUGGLE BETWEEN DREYER'S WORDS AND IMAGES OPEN US UP TO THE REAL?

Father" orally from her mother), she scrawls a hesitant "X" at the bottom of the page; but the judges, deeming this mark insufficient, are unsatisfied. Loyseleur approaches, and, placing his hand over hers, guides her fingers in the writing of her name, after which she adds an enigmatic "O."[11] The signature looms enormously on the screen, a bold image of the depths to which Joan has fallen. Joan will of course soon rise from that fall, renouncing her signature, but thus ensuring her death at the hands of the authorities. This is why, too, the great, secret crisis that ended Gertrud's one true romance takes the shape of her discovery of Lidman's words on the drawing depicting herself; Gertrud's graphophobia is not simply a consistent though idiosyncratic trait throughout the film (and throughout the life of her "real" self, Maria von Platen), it is a thoroughly coherent mark of her shared identity with Joan, with Mary, and with Charcot's (and Nygren's) women with the "sixth sense."

Joan's and Gertrud's renunciation of and assault on the word reveal to us Dreyer's bold strategy for deconstructing the feminine/masculine, Imaginary/ Symbolic impasse of both the tradition from which he emerges and the criticism that has attempted to explain him. Joan's mark and Gertrud's tearing enact a short-circuit in the Imaginary/Symbolic exchange, an interruption we have seen described as the "excessive" image in *Joan* and *Gertrud*, or what Linderman calls the "uncoded image," images that mean and don't mean. They function as what Jacques Lacan has called a *sinthom*. A sinthom, according to Lacan, is not a legible Freudian symptom, but neither is it a mark of a pure negativity or intelligibility. As Slavoj Žižek explains it, "in contrast to symptom which is a cipher of some repressed meaning, sinthom has no determinate meaning; it just gives body, in its repetitive pattern, to some elementary matrix of jouissance, of excessive enjoyment. Although sinthoms do not have sense, they do radiate *jouis*-sense, enjoy-meant."[12]

---

11 Loyseleur, of course, is already well known to us as a forger; he had earlier tricked Joan with a faked letter from King Charles. We might well ask how an illiterate person could be fooled by a forgery, but Joan, like Dreyer, understands the power of the signature as far more than a simple signifier.

12 Slavoj Žižek, *Enjoy Your Symptom! Jacques Lacan in Hollywood and Out*, (New York: Routledge, 2001), 199.

The sinthom marks a postmodern textuality that Žižek understands to be the result of a more direct encounter with the "real." And it is this "realism" that rings so true to Dreyer's work. Allow me to quote at some length from Žižek:

Postmodernism thus accomplishes a kind of shift of perspective in relation to modernism: what in modernism appeared as the subversive margin—symptoms in which the repressed truth of the "false" totality emerges—is now displaced into the very heart, as the hard core of the Real that different attempts of symbolization endeavor in vain to integrate and to "gentrify". . . . The theoretical antagonism thus shifts from the axis Imaginary-Symbolic to the axis Symbolic-Real: the aim of the modernist "symptomal reading" is to ferret out the texture of discursive (symbolic) practices whose imaginary effect is the substantial totality, whereas postmodernism focuses on the traumatic Thing which resists symbolization (symbolic practices).[13]

The shift from the axis Imaginary-Symbolic to the axis Symbolic-Real is the movement that enables Dreyer to so insistently (and seemingly paradoxically) proclaim the authenticity of the text *and* the authenticity of the "real" self that resists the text. The locus of this paradox is the "traumatic Thing," which in *Gertrud* is in so many ways Gertrud herself: Dreyer makes full use of her repeated rejection of the Symbolic order, and her final hermit-like solitude, to bring to life, like Joan, "the subjective position of the saint, i.e., of an objectival remainder-excrement . . . a falling out of the object from the symbolic network, the assumption of a distance from the symbolic universe."[14] (Gertrud's removal is from this perspective structurally identical with the "falling out" from the symbolic network of Dreyer's birth mother, herself a "remainder-excrement" whose absence was required in order for her illegitimate son to assume the name of a father, even if that name was an assumed identity.)

The production of this subject-object is the result of what Žižek calls, following F.W.J. Schelling, an "Act," which he understands as "the moment when

13 Ibid., 123.

14 Ibid., 42.

the subject who is its bearer *suspends* the network of symbolic fictions which serve as a support of his daily life and confronts again the radical negativity upon which they are founded."[15] The "act" in this sense is a confrontation with the radical negativity that lies beneath the "false" totality of the symbolic order, but this confrontation is not itself a simple negation. Žižek sees the "act" as paradigmatically "feminine," but its performance does not banish the feminine to the realm of the insignificant; rather, it places the feminine actively on the side of the "real," of a constitutive excess that opens the human subject to a space of experience beyond the confines of the Symbolic.[16]

We have already noted at length the torturous aspects of Dreyer's textual practice, the ways in which the infliction of pain and the creation of meaning in his texts appear to go hand in hand, as they do so spectacularly in *Gertrud*'s tapestry. This is of a piece with his particular realism; one could understand, following Freud, that the replacement of the "pleasure principle" by the "reality principle" requires an unpleasant recognition by the human subject of the realities of the world, a recognition by which the subject learns to "adjust" or give up its demands to those of social and physical "reality." In Freud, the principle

---

15 Ibid., 53.

16 Žižek again: "[W]e shouldn't forget that the paradigmatic case of such an act is feminine: Antigone's 'No!' to Creon, to state power; her act is literally suicidal, she excludes herself from the community. . . . Perhaps we should then risk the hypothesis that, according to its inherent logic, the act as real is 'feminine,' in contrast to the 'masculine' performative" (*Enjoy Your Symptom!*, 46). In light of this argument, we should understand the title of the chapter in Žižek's book in which it appears—"Why is *Woman* a Symptom of Man?"—as underscoring the "lack" of prior Lacanian theories of the feminine. The feminine, when aligned not with the symptom but with the sinthom, is no longer understood simply as a symptom of the masculine. See also Žižek's essay on Friedrich Wilhelm Joseph Schelling's *Ages of the World*, where he discusses the "radical negativity" of Schelling's feminine "Ground," which serves as "the foundation of the male Word. . . . It is easy to recognize [in Schelling] the standard patriarchal fear of the destructive force of fully asserted femininity. There is, however, another, perhaps unexpected conclusion to be drawn from this: is this radical negativity bent on destroying every determinate Existence not the very kernel of subjectivity? Does this not mean that subjectivity is, in its most basic dimension, in an unheard-of way, 'feminine'?" Slavoj Žižek and F. W. J. von Schelling, *The Abyss of Freedom/Ages of the World*, trans. Judith Norman (Ann Arbor: University of Michigan Press, 1997), 8. Žižek here turns the Kristevan conundrum (of the feminine's insignificance) on its head.

of pleasure, in bowing to that of reality, produces a pain that is a sign of the self's acceptance of the Real.

Access to the Real requires the trauma of the collision of the pleasure principle with the reality principle, and in Lacan's version of the subject's opening to the real we can understand the sinthom as the mark this trauma leaves on the subject. But for Lacan and Žižek, the traumatic intrusion of the "Real" is not simply the imposition from outside of a force that violently suppresses the self's primal demand for satisfaction; it is a constitutive aspect of the self's own formation. Žižek argues, thus, that there is a "*positive* dimension" to this impediment: true, it "prevents the circle of pleasure from closing, it introduces an irreducible displeasure, but the psychic apparatus finds a sort of perverse pleasure *in this displeasure itself*, in the never-ending, repeated circulation around the unattainable, always missed object. The Lacanian name for this 'pleasure in pain' is of course enjoyment (*jouissance*)."[17]

Dreyer's much-vaunted "sadism" is therefore not simply a personal predilection, added idiosyncratically to his film texts; it is a defining feature of the work his texts perform, allowing for the "pleasure in displeasure" that is the mark for him of access to reality. Dreyer's realism is the realism of the Real, a realism that is also spiritual, as it resides within the self as a rupture or break within the "closed" circle of the pleasure principle.

But we still have one important question to answer before we can neatly wrap up our account of Dreyer's "Real-ism" so tightly within this Lacanian framework. That question concerns, finally, the role in Dreyer's work of language, of the symbolic itself, as the agency by which this disturbance within the psychic apparatus clears a path to the Real. We saw in the iconography of the Annunciation how the "self-contained balance" of the Virgin's world was disturbed by the entry of the Word into the virginal, enclosed garden of her being, an entry that broke open and destabilized the space of her—and of humanity's—experience. In the course of hundreds of years of depictions of that scene, the visible "hybrid space" of word and body, which was a constitutive

17 Žižek, *Enjoy Your Symptom!* 48.

element of the representation of the scene, gave way to ever more "realistic" representations—depictions that emphasized the internal emotional aspects of Mary's violent and sexualized responses to the coming of the Word. These representations finally can be seen to have for all intents and purposes collapsed into the identical poses of the early modern hysterical woman, the privileged site of the "symptom," that is, of the exterior readability of the interior incarnation of language in the body, as that language, in Freud, is claimed by the subject herself as the story of her own, internal trauma. Now comes Dreyer, who extends the "realism" of the depiction of this encounter between body and word by insisting that the traumatic, interior rupture created by the incarnation of the Word can never be healed or closed, that it is just this rupture that *is* our reality. Dreyer can thus simultaneously insist on the "spiritual realism" of his work while also claiming a pure textual authority for the "skanseslöse realisme"—the "merciless realism," as he called it—of his images.

Who, I ask, more than any other film character, has enacted with precision the painful enjoyment of the self's access to reality? Gertrud.

And so we can identify the "emptiness" Bordwell saw at *Gertrud*'s center with the fullness and plenitude of the film's aesthetic, an often violent rendering (of text, of narrative, of image) that marks the mutilating rupture created by Gertrud's "act," her refusal of others and their compromised love, her commitment, in the name of an impossible love, to divorce not marriage. Gertrud, like Joan, figures as an excess to the narrative that tries to tell her story, an excess once again born of the conflict between image and word, and rendered, in more ways than one, by the image of the dogs tearing into the woman looming on the tapestry behind her, and by the fissure of the woman's sex into which the narrative gaze is invited to vanish.[18]

18 As I was completing this book, I discovered Brigitte Peucker's just-published *The Material Image: Art and the Real in Film* (Palo Alto: Stanford University Press, 2007). Building on work she began in *Incorporating Images: Film and the Rival Arts* (Princeton: Princeton University Press, 1997), Peucker gives a number of fine readings centered around the way art and works of art function as points of access to the real in film, judiciously mobilizing a wide array of theoretical frameworks, from Lacanian theory to cognitive approaches. Anyone who has read this far will be delighted to continue the journey with Peucker's work.

In the end, Gertrud's (and Dreyer's) "powerful attack on significance"[19] (in the words of David Bordwell) is not made in the name of the image, and Gertrud's (and Dreyer's) iconoclasm is not performed in the name of the Word: rather, their struggle is on behalf of the Real, of that which is torn open in and for us when text and image render each other.

I hope that, in these few pages, I have cleared even a small opening through which we might gaze on the terrible greatness of Dreyer's, and Gertrud's, sublime failure. The tearing by language of the body into its readable expression is, in Dreyer, as in de Sade, the index of a deadly serious anxiety about the adequacy of writing and of representation in general to express the self at its moment of purest consciousness—a consciousness in the realist tradition that is paradoxically an awareness of the self's own textuality.

I hope, too, that this little book will inspire students of Dreyer to return to his films with a renewed sense of awe—indeed, of awe at the prospect of our own sublime failure ever fully to "read" them. And if I have managed here to write anything *but* a monograph about *Gertrud*, it is in part because Dreyer himself teaches us that even a single image, or moment, can open up so huge and dynamic a network of references and meanings that sometimes our best response should be, in deference to and in imitation of Dreyer's own mania for research, a similar mania, born of the never-ending quest to live and to create in the company of the Real. Regard, again, Gertrud. She is all, as Philostratus would say, from Dreyer. And yet she no longer follows him.

19 Bordwell, *Films of Carl-Theodor Dreyer*, 188.

CREDITS

Gertrud
Denmark. 1964. Palladium

Director   **CARL THEODOR DREYER**
Screenplay   **CARL THEODOR DREYER**
Based on the play *Gertrud*   by Hjalmar Söderberg (1906)
Assistant directors   **SOLVEIG ERSGAARD, JENS RAVN**
Poems by   **GRETHE RISBJERG THOMSEN**
Cinematographer   **HENNING BENDTSEN**
Sound   **KNUD KRISTENSEN**
Production design   **KAI RASCH**
Costumes   **BERIT NYKJÆR**
Costume assistant   **WILLY BERG HAUSEN**
Gertrud's gowns   **FABIELLE**
Gertrud's hats   **WINNIE**
Men's wardrobe   **M.G. RASMUSSEN**
Editor   **EDITH SCHLÜSSEL**
Composer   **JØRGEN JERSILD**
Conductor   **PETER WILLEMOES**
Lighting   **OVE HANSEN**
Color timing   **JOHAN ANKERSTJERNE A/S**
Makeup   **BODIL OVERBYE**

CAST

Gertrud **NINA PENS RODE**
Gustav Kanning **BENDT ROTHE**
Gabriel Lidman **EBBE RODE**
Erland Jansson **BAARD OWE**
Axel Nygren **AXEL STRØBYE**
Madam Kanning **ANNA MALBERG**

with

KARL GUSTAV AHLEFELDT

VERA GEBUR

CARL JOHN HVIID

WILLIAM KNOBLAUCH

LARS KNUTZON

EDOUARD MIELCHE

World premiere Paris, 18 December 1964
Length 111 minutes

Filmed at Hellerup Studios and Vallø Castle Park, summer 1964

BIBLIOGRAPHY

Abel, Richard. *The French Cinema: The First Wave, 1915–1929*. Princeton: Princeton University Press, 1984.

Alberti, Leon B. *On Painting*. Translated by Cecil Grayson. New York: Penguin, 1991.

Alpers, Svetlana. "Ekphrasis and Aesthetic Attitudes in Vasari's *Lives*." *Journal of the Warburg and Courtald Institutes* 23 (1960): 190–215.

Andrews, Lew. *Story and Space in Renaissance Art: The Rebirth of Continuous Narrative*. Cambridge: Cambridge University Press, 1998.

Baxandall, Michael. *Painting and Experience in Fifteenth-Century Italy*. Oxford: Oxford University Press, 1972.

Bazin, André. *What is Cinema?* Vol. 1. Translated by Hugh Gray. Berkeley: University of California Press, 2004. First published 1967 by University of California Press.

Boccaccio, Giovanni. *Decameron*. Edited by Vittore Branca. Turin: Einaudi, 1980.

Bordwell, David. *The Films of Carl-Theodor Dreyer*. Berkeley: University of California Press, 1981.

Bryson, Norman. *Art and Text in Ancient Greek Culture*. Edited by Simon Goldhill and Robin Osborne. Cambridge: Cambridge University Press, 1994.

Burch, Noel. "Carl Theodor Dreyer: The Major Phase." In *Cinema: A Critical Dictionary*, edited by Richard Roud, 296–310. New York: Nationwide Book Services, 1980.

Callman, Ellen. "The Growing Threat to Marital Bliss as Seen in Fifteenth-Century Florentine Paintings." *Studies in Iconography* 5 (1979): 73–92.

Cardile, Paul J. "Observations on the Iconography of Leonardo da Vinci's Uffizi Annunciation." *Studies in Iconography* 7, no. 8 (1981–82): 189–208.

Carrier, David. "Ekphrasis and Interpretation: Two Modes of Art History Writing." *British Journal of Aesthetics* 27 (1987): 20–31.

Caws, Mary Ann. "The Annunciation of a Text: Rilke and the Birth of the Poem." In *The Eye in the Text*, 104–21. Princeton: Princeton University Press, 1981.

Charcot, Jean-Martin. *Charcot the Clinician: The Tuesday Lessons*. Translated by Christopher G. Goetz. New York: Raven Press, 1987.

———. *Leçons du Mardi a la Salpetriere: Policliniques 1887–1888. Notes de cours de MM. Blin, Charcot, et Colin*. Paris: M. Delahaye et Emile Lecrosnier, 1887.

———. *Lectures on the Diseases of the Nervous System*. Translated by George Sigerson. Philadelphia: Henry C. Lea, 1879.

Clover, Carol. *Men, Women, and Chain Saws: Gender in the Modern Horror Film*. Princeton: Princeton University Press, 1993.

Copjec, Joan. "Flavit et Dissipati Sunt." In *October: The First Decade, 1976–1986*, edited by Annette Michelsen et al., 296–316. Cambridge: MIT Press, 1987.

Cruise, Colin. "Versions of the Annunciation: Wilde's Aestheticism and the Message of Beauty." In *After the Pre-Raphaelites: Art and Aestheticism in Victorian England*, edited by Elizabeth Prettejohn, 167–87. Rutgers: Rutgers University Press, 1999.

de Lauretis, Theresa. *Alice Doesn't*. Bloomington: Indiana University Press, 1984.

Denny, Don. *The Annunciation from the Right from Early Christian Times to the Sixteenth Century*. New York: Garland, 1977.

Didi-Huberman, Georges. *Invention de l'hysterie*. Paris: Macula, 1982.

Dreyer, Carl T. *Four Screenplays*. Translated by Oliver Stallybrass. Bloomington: Indiana University Press, 1970.

———. *Oeuvres Cinématographiques 1926-1934*. Edited by Maurice Drouzy and Charles Tesson. Paris: Cinématheque française, 1983.

———. *Tommen: Carl Th. Dreyersjournalistiske virksomhed*. Edited by Peter Schepelern. Copenhagen: C. A. Reitzels Forlag, 1982.

Drouzy, Maurice. *Carl Th. Dreyer né Nilsson*. Paris: Cerf, 1982.

———. *Kildemateriale til en biografi om Carl Th. Dreyer*. Copenhagen: C. A. Reitzels Forlag, 1982.

Drum, Jean, and Dale Drum. *My Only Great Passion: The Life and Films of Carl Th. Dreyer*. London: Scarecrow Press, 2000.

Egholm, Morten. "The innovative and wilful [sic] adaptor: What Carl Th. Dreyer did to Hjalmar Söderberg's *Gertrud*." *TijdSchrift voor Skandinavistiek* 27, no. 2 (2006). http://dpc.uba.uva.nl/tvs/vol27/nro2/arto9 (accessed August 27, 2007).

Frankenberry, Nancy. Review of *Nature's Self: Our Journey from Origin to Spirit*, by Robert S. Corrington. *Journal of the American Academy of Religion* 66, no. 1 (Spring 1998): 171–173.

Freud, Sigmund, and Joseph Breuer. *Studies on Hysteria*. Translated by James Strachey and Alex Strachey. New York: Penguin, 1974.

Heffernan, James. *Museum of Words: The Poetics of Ekphrasis from Homer to Ashbery*. Chicago: University of Chicago Press, 1993.

Hickey, Dave. *The Invisible Dragon: Four Essays on Beauty*. Los Angeles: Art Issues Press, 1994.

Hirn, Yrjo. *The Sacred Shrine: A Study of the Poetry and Art of the Catholic Church*. Boston, Beacon Press, 1957.

Holly, Michael A. "Witnessing an Annunciation." In *Past Looking: Historical Imagination and the Rhetoric of the Image*, 149–69. Ithaca: Cornell University Press, 1996.

Janet, Pierre. *Major Symptoms of Hysteria*. New York: Macmillan, 1920.

Jay, Martin. *Downcast Eyes: The Denigration of Vision in Twentieth-Century French Thought*. Berkeley: University of California Press, 1993.

Kant, Immanuel. *The Critique of Judgement*. Translated by James Creed Meredith. 100ff. Oxford: Oxford University Press, 1952.

Kau, Edvin. *Dreyers filmkunst*. Copenhagen: Akademisk Forlag, 1989.

Kristeva, Julia. *Desire in Language: A Semiotic Approach to Literature and Art*. Translated by Thomas Gora, Alice Jardin, and Leon S. Roudiez. New York: Columbia University Press, 1980.

"La Passion de Jeanne d'Arc." Special issue, *Avant-Scène du Cinéma*, nos. 367–368 (1988).

Lessing, Gotthold Ephraim. *Laocoon: An Essay on the Limits of Painting and Poetry*. Translated by Edward Allen McCormick. Baltimore: Johns Hopkins University Press, 1766.

Linderman, Deborah. "Uncoded Images in the Heterogeneous Text." *Wide Angle* 3, no. 3 (1980): 34–41. Reprinted in *Narrative, Apparatus, Ideology*, edited by Philip Rosen, 143–52. New York: Columbia University Press, 1986. Page references are to the 1980 edition.

Mälarstedt, Kurt. *Ett liv på egna villkor*. Stockholm: Wallström & Widstrand, 2006.

Olsen, Christine. "Gross Expenditure: Botticelli's Nastagio degli Onesti Panels." *Studies in Iconography* 5 (1979): 146–70.

Panofsky, Erwin. *Studies in Iconology: Humanistic Themes in the Art of the Renaissance*. New York: Westview Press, 2001.

Peucker, Brigette. *Incorporating Images: Film and the Rival Arts*. Princeton: Princeton University Press, 1997.

———. *The Material Image: Art and the Real in Film*. Palo Alto: Stanford University Press, 2007.

Philostratus the Elder, Philostratus the Younger, and Callistratus. *Imagines*. Translated by Arthur Fairbanks. New York: Putnam, 1931.

Purtle, Carol J. *The Marian Paintings of Jan van Eyck*. Princeton: Princeton University Press, 1982.

Réau, Louis. *Iconographie de l'art Chretien*. Vol. 1. Paris: Presses Universitaires de France, 1957.

Rein, Sten. *Hjalmar Soderbergs* Gertrud*: Studier kring ettkarleksdrama*. Stockholm: Bonniers, 1962.

Robb, David M. "The Iconography of the Annunciation in the Fourteenth and Fifteenth Centuries." *Art Bulletin* 18 (1936): 480–526.

Rose, Jacqueline. "Dora: Fragment of an Analysis." In *In Dora's Case: Freud—Hysteria—Feminism*, edited by Charles Bernheimer, 128–48. New York: Columbia University Press, 1990.

Rosenbaum, Jonathan. "Gertrud: The Desire for the Image." *Sight and Sound* 55, no. 1 (Winter 1985–1986): 40.

Schamus, James. "Dreyer's Textual Realism." In *Carl Dreyer*, edited by Jyette Jensen, 123–28. New York: Museum of Modern Art, 1989.

Schiller, Gertrud. *Iconography of Christian Art*. Translated by Janet Seligman. Greenwich: New York Graphic Society, 1971.

Schrader, Paul. *Transcendental Style in Film: Ozu, Bresson, Dreyer*. Cambridge, MA: Da Capo Press, 1988.

Scott, Grant F. "The Rhetoric of Dilation: Ekphrasis and Ideology." *Word and Image* 7, no. 4 (1991): 302.

Silverman, Kaja. "The Fragments of a Fashionable Discourse." In *Studies in Entertainment: Critical Approaches to Mass Culture*, edited by Tania Modaleski, 139–52. Bloomington: Indiana University Press, 1986.

Söderberg, Hjalmar. *The Serious Game*. Translated by Eva Claeson. London: Marion Boyars, 2001.

Spencer, John R. "Spatian Imagery of the Annunciation in Fifteenth Century Florence." *The Art Bulletin* 37 (1955): 273–80.

Strindberg, August. *Selected Plays*. Translated by Evert Sprinchorn. Minneapolis: University of Minnesota Press, 1986.

Téchiné, André. "La Parole de la Fin." *Cahiers du cinéma* 164 (March 1965): 72.

Veith, Ilza. *Hysteria: The History of a Disease*. Chicago: University of Chicago Press, 1965.

Virgil. *The Aeneid*. Translated by Robert Fagles. New York: Viking, 2006.

Warner, Marina. *Alone of All Her Sex: The Myth and the Cult of the Virgin Mary*. New York: Alfred A. Knopf, 1976.

Webb, Ruth. "Ekphrasis Ancient and Modern: The Invention of a Genre." *Word and Image* 15 (1999): 7–18.

Williams, Linda. *Hard Core: Power, Pleasure, and the "Frenzy of the Visible."* Berkeley: University of California Press, 1999.

Wolf, Bryan. "Confessions of a Closet Ekphrastic." *Yale Journal of Criticism* 3, no. 3 (1990): 181–203.

Žižek, Slavoj, and F. W. J. von Schelling. *The Abyss of Freedom/Ages of the World*. Translated by Judith Norman. Ann Arbor: University of Michigan Press, 1997.

———. *Enjoy Your Symptom! Jacques Lacan in Hollywood and Out*. New York: Routledge, 2001.

INDEX

Illustrations are indicated by page numbers in italics.